Schools with *Spirit*

Nurturing the Inner Lives of Children and Teachers

Edited by

Linda Lantieri

Beacon Press BOSTON

Beacon Press
25 Beacon Street
Boston, Massachusetts 02108-2892
www.beacon.org

Beacon Press books
are published under the auspices of
the Unitarian Universalist Association of Congregations.

06 05 04 03 02 01   8 7 6 5 4 3 2 1

"Now I Become Myself," from *Collected Poems 1930–1993* by May Sarton.
Copyright © 1993, 1988, 1984, 1980, 1974 by May Sarton. Used by permission
of W. W. Norton & Company, Inc.

This book is printed on acid-free paper that meets the uncoated paper
ANSI/NISO specifications for permanence as revised in 1992.

LIBRARY OF CONGRESS CATALOGING-IN-PUBLICATION DATA
Schools with spirit : nurturing the inner lives of children and teachers
/ edited by Linda Lantieri.
      p.   cm.
Includes bibliographical references.
    ISBN 0-8070-3132-1 (hardcover : alk. paper)
    1. Teaching—Religious aspects. 2. School children—Religious life.
3. Teachers—Religious life. 4. Spiritual life. I. Lantieri, Linda.
    LB1027.2 .S36 2001
    372.1102—dc21   00-012994

*T*his book is dedicated to

my mother, whose life rich in purpose and meaning taught me that what matters most is to live my soul's calling,

and

my father, whose life, death, and faith taught me that God is never far away.

Contents

Foreword

DANIEL GOLEMAN

*O*ver the last five years or so since the publication of my book *Emotional Intelligence*, I've watched with satisfaction the spread of programs in social and emotional learning in schools across America and around the world. Such courses had already begun to sprout up in schools here and there by the time I wrote my book; its publication played a role in catalyzing and energizing that movement.

Now *Schools with Spirit* seems to signal the emergence of another significant movement in educating our young people, one that speaks to a crucial dimension in children's lives: the search for meaning and purpose. This new focus moves some of the key elements of emotional intelligence into a deeper dimension. Self-awareness takes on a new depth of inner exploration; managing emotions becomes self-discipline; empathy becomes a basis for altruism, caring, and compassion. And all of these basic skills for life can now be seen as building blocks of character.

The search for meaning, of course, has traditionally fallen within the orbit of church and synagogue, mosque and temple. Not everyone will agree that nurturing the inner life of children has a place in a school's mission. But what's proposed here is not that we bring any particular creed or religious belief to children—the Constitution's separation of church and state clearly prohibits that, at least in our public schools.

But *Schools with Spirit* is about opening the way for teaching children to value having a spiritual life, whatever it may be. As such it should find readers among those who teach in Sunday schools or schools sponsored by religious groups as well as anyone who would teach in a "school with spirit."

Schools with spirit of any variety welcome students' deeper questions, and teach in a way that encourages their spiritual quest. For those who teach a mix of students, that quest can be supported whatever direction it may take, without offering a fixed set of answers.

Linda Lantieri and the other contributors to this book explore here how schools can nurture children's hearts and souls as well as their minds. This exploration marks a promising beginning for a common search among educators who seek to find what it means to teach "the whole child." In drawing together the thoughtful voices of those who share these concerns, she has done a favor for all of us who want to help children cultivate their spiritual lives.

Preface

LINDA LANTIERI

Schools with Spirit is dedicated to all children who would benefit from having their inner lives more present in our classrooms and to the adults who have the courage to help evoke that change. A bold new vision for our schools is needed—one that reclaims them as soulful places of learning where the spiritual dimension is welcomed. This book is about the possibilities and practicalities of creating such a movement and the role you and I can play in it.

I've always considered it a great blessing that my occupation and my vocation have coincided—that my professional life has also been my calling. For more than three decades now, I have worked in the field of public education. I have worn many hats: classroom teacher, school administrator, education activist, college faculty member. For the past sixteen years I've served as the director of one of our country's largest and most successful efforts to teach social and emotional skills in the classroom—the Resolving Conflict Creatively Program (RCCP) of Educators for Social Responsibility. Throughout my career, I have always felt that the education of young people involved not only their intellectual, emotional, and social development but also their spiritual growth. However, I never could have imagined that what I would be called upon to do next would be to build a bridge between the inner life of mind and spirit and the outer world of secular education. This challenge is not an easy one to meet, because our society has built an almost impenetrable wall between the two.

When I began teaching in a fifth grade classroom in East Harlem in 1968, I was only twenty years old. I couldn't even vote in the presidential election and yet I was entrusted with nurturing the minds, hearts, and *souls* of thirty-seven children. My training for this task was barely adequate in many ways, but one thing I did know for certain: I was to remember the First Amendment's separation of church and state. I don't recall a time when any education professor or school official actually went over the specifics of what this meant, but it seemed to me at the time that I was forbidden to discuss with my students a vital source of purpose and meaning in my own life. I had been raised in a faith-based home and my spiritual experience was and is still a central and defining aspect of my life. It was this part of me, I concluded, that was not welcome in my classroom and my teaching. And so my very rewarding life as a teacher was also a divided one—a life of not being able, to paraphrase the words of Parker Palmer, to live on the outside the truth I knew on the inside. I realize in hindsight that as long as I was fully present with those thirty-seven children, which happened often, my inner life was being expressed. But it didn't feel that way at the time, and I suspect many others serving in secular schools know what I'm talking about.

I was asking myself the most basic of questions: What am I doing here? What are the unique gifts that are mine to share with this group of students? I soon noticed that the students at P.S. 171 were often confronting deep questions as well. Depending on how old they were, they were even asking them out loud—among the youngest their spirituality was still integrated enough into their lives that they hadn't yet learned to repress it. A six-year-old boy named Jason came up to me in the lunchroom during the first week of school and asked me, "Where did my grandmother go when she died?" I remember saying something like, "Maybe you should ask your mother. We can talk about it sometime, but not now." I now regret that I didn't say, "That's an interesting question, Jason. I also wonder about that. What do *you* think?" As a fifth grade teacher, though, I didn't often hear this kind of question from my own students. By the time they were nine or ten, it seemed, young people's inner lives had gone underground. They too had learned to live this "divided life."

In public school classrooms today, the sacred is intentionally absent because we decided many years ago that nurturing the inner life was not the business of public education, and so both children and teachers have had to leave their deeper questions about the mysteries of life at home. I have spent the last several years in the field of public education struggling with what it would mean to live "divided no more." What might it really look like to have every major thread of my experience woven into my vocation, my life's tapestry?

Is it possible for schools to nurture the hearts and spirits of students in ways that do not violate the beliefs of families or the constitutional principle of the separation of church and state? Although this is a difficult question to answer, many educators are beginning to acknowledge that teaching the whole child *can* include welcoming the wisdom of a child's soul into our classrooms. The original intent of the First Amendment was to protect our nation from the establishment of any specific religion or dogma while giving all citizens the right to freely express their own beliefs. It certainly was never meant to suffocate such an important part of life as our spiritual experience.

But how this aspect of human experience can be addressed in public schools is still a thorny matter. This book, although it presents diverse perspectives, is not about having all the answers. It's far too early for that. Instead, we who have contributed to the discussion here are sharing with the reader "the fruits of our contemplations," as Thomas Aquinas put it.

I do know that bringing forth a book about welcoming the spiritual dimension into public schools is risky. I am well aware of how far I am deviating from the status quo. Indeed, numerous well-meaning colleagues have tried to warn me against doing so, and I've thought long and hard about rocking the boat. Luckily I've had a little practice. In the 1980s and 1990s, we wouldn't have imagined that public schools would embrace the teaching of conflict resolution or emotional intelligence as a normal, natural part of the curriculum, yet I've spent the last decade playing my part in making that happen. So I'm no stranger to mustering up the courage to say and do what I know in my heart will be better for children and teachers. I take inspiration from one of my heroes, Dr. Lorraine Monroe, a New York City principal who says, "Let the battle scars become beauty marks."

I take this risk because I strongly feel that the dilemmas of our times are deeply spiritual ones that our children need to be prepared to meet. The high-profile incidents of violence in our schools over the past several years have shared some common characteristics. These seemingly "senseless" events, including multiple murders linked to attempts at suicide by the perpetrators, have often occurred in places where young people possessed too many things that had too little meaning. Material wealth did not seem to satisfy their deeper hunger for what feeds the soul. And yet most of our young people growing up today, from the poorest to the most affluent, are imprisoned by our obsession as a culture with material things. They get the message early on that to feel good about themselves or to feel the love of their family, they need to own the latest Star Wars toy, designer sneakers, or a fancy car. We are teaching our children by our example that we should look to the outside for meaning, not the inside. We are, in Dr. King's words, "judging success by the index of our salaries or the size of our automobiles rather than by the quality of our service and our relationship to humanity."

By not welcoming the sacred, "that which is worthy of respect," as Parker Palmer defines it, our schools run the risk of raising a whole generation of young people who will be bereft of the wisdom and connectedness they need to live a fully human life.

Having been in the field of violence prevention in schools for so many years, I'm concerned that we don't make the same mistake twice. Amid the social crises of the 1980s and 1990s, we waited for young people to really get in trouble, even kill each other, before we responded with programs to create safe schools. I hope we have learned from that past not to wait for more and more young people to lose their sense of meaning and purpose before we invite soul into education.

Webster's describes "spirit" as the "animating or vital principle held to give life." It is the spiritual dimension of our lives that helps us place our actions in a wider, richer context. I am only one of a number of educators, social scientists, and concerned citizens who are beginning to explore the role of public schools in nurturing a broader, deeper vision that takes us beyond ourselves and gives us and our actions a sense of worth in the context of community.

For me, this vision has deep roots in a very specific experience and history. The Resolving Conflict Creatively Program, which I cofounded in 1985, started as a joint initiative of Educators for Social Responsibility Metropolitan Area (ESR Metro) and the New York City Board of Education. Today, under the auspices of Educators for Social Responsibility's national office, I serve as the director of a very successful research-based K-12 school program that is now reaching more than four hundred schools in eight states, with beginnings in Brazil, England, and Puerto Rico. From the very start, our aim was to create caring, safe school communities in a society that seemed to be giving up on children, abandoning them to a climate of perpetual violence.

Over the years, as we worked with teachers, administrators, young people, and parents, I started to notice that sometimes our efforts reached beyond our goals of equipping children and adolescents with practical skills in conflict resolution. The kind of insightful thinking and courageous behavior that some of our young people exhibited seemed to be more than the byproduct of a good prevention program.

When I first met Eugene he had been a peer mediator for several years in his South Bronx high school (training students as peer mediators was and is a key component of the Resolving Conflict Creatively Program). Once, when he was asked by his teacher to think about a goal he had for himself in the future, he had said, "To be alive at twenty-one." He was eighteen years old at the time. A year after he graduated, I got a telephone call from his principal telling me that Eugene had been in the "wrong place at the wrong time" and had been hit by a random bullet while standing on a street corner in his neighborhood. He was in Metropolitan Hospital, paralyzed from the waist down. It took me two days to get up enough courage to visit him.

As I walked into the hospital ward that day I saw a disheartening sight—over thirty young men in wheelchairs, many of them victims of the violence that plagued our city. I spotted Eugene immediately. I asked him, "How are you doing?" I will never forget his response. He said, "I wasn't doing too great until this morning, when I got up and decided to find the place in my heart that could forgive the guy that pulled the trigger." Almost speechless, I managed to ask, "How were you able to do that?" He replied, "I realized that I could have been that guy if I didn't know there was a better way."

The compassion and insight that Eugene displayed that day is still the exception, not the norm, in our work with RCCP. But it has inspired me to think further about how to foster such resilience and courage in our young people and how we can make these exceptions in students' and teachers' lives more widespread.

Schools with Spirit gives voice to a group of educators and youth workers who are providing the young people they serve with opportunities for experiences and meaningful dialogue that truly feed what I would call their souls but others might term their inner lives. The authors of each chapter show how they have managed to nurture the inner life of their students while respecting their diverse religious beliefs and cultures. They are not doing religious education, nor are they exposing students to devotional practices. They are a network of individuals who have found exciting and powerful ways to attend to what I would call the spiritual life of young people while respecting both the religious convictions of some students and the more secular worldview shared by others.

Some of the contributors to *Schools with Spirit* talk about aesthetic experiences—the pleasure and meaning to be found in creating or appreciating a work of art. Others speak of connectedness to people and to nature as being among the most meaningful aspects of our lives. Some discuss new ideas about social and emotional development and cognitive psychology. Many touch on the importance of teachers learning to nurture their own inner lives.

Nancy Carlsson-Paige asks us to create early childhood classrooms that honor the spirit by honoring the whole child. Rachael Kessler presents seven "gateways to the soul" and guides us as teachers in developing a way of being in the classroom that can support the spiritual search of adolescence. Jacob Needleman talks about what he learned about young people's quest for meaning from teaching philosophy at a local high school in California. Martin Brokenleg and Larry Brendtro show us we have much to learn from Native American peoples concerning the inner lives of children, and introduce us to a model being used in many schools, the Circle of Courage. Laura Parker Roerden explores how time spent in nature can refresh and inspire us, and presents ideas for how to construct school programs in which the experience of nature is integral to the curriculum. Zephryn Conte reminds us that the arts can be a transformative tool for honoring young people's inner lives and for fostering self-knowledge and personal growth. Angeles Arrien presents a model for teachers' deep engagement—a vision of how to lead a life of quality and integrity drawn from various cultural traditions. Parker Palmer, Marcy Jackson, Rick Jackson, and David Sluyter explore ways to nurture teachers' souls. Finally, Geoffrey Canada eloquently describes how training in the philosophy and practice of the martial arts can be a powerful anchor for children caught in the crossfire of our violent culture.

I am grateful for the diversity of perspectives and backgrounds among my colleagues, and for their courage in sharing their questions as well as their convictions. They serve as an inspiration to all of us who are advocating for soul in education—for schools with spirit. One of the most powerful things we can do in creating this new vision is to connect with others to help us remember we are not alone. We are beginning a movement.

Schools with Spirit

Integral Life, Integral Teacher: An Interview with Parker J. Palmer

*T*his conversation with Parker J. Palmer first appeared in *Yes! A Journal of Positive Futures* (winter 1998/99).

INTERVIEWER: One of the things that I found very striking about your work is the idea that the simple choice to live with integrity can have far-reaching effects. What experiences brought you to believe that this was such a central issue?

PALMER: What I know about living a divided life starts with my training as an academic. I was taught to keep things in airtight compartments: to keep my ideas apart from my feelings, because ideas were reliable but feelings were not; to keep my theories apart from my actions, because the theory can be pure, but the action is always sullied.

For the teachers I meet around the country, the decision to live divided-no-more means teaching in a way that corresponds to the truth that they know, rather than according to the latest pedagogical fad or to whatever pressures the institution may be putting on them.

These are teachers, for example, who are integrating emotional work with cognitive work in the classroom. Certainly in higher education, there's a real taboo against doing that. These teachers are choosing to take the significant risks that come with going against the taboo because they know from their own experience that the mind and the heart can't be separated.

An example of that is the work of Sheila Tobias and others who have helped young women learn mathematics by dealing not just with the intellect, but with the emotional paralysis that many young women have felt about math. By addressing that message at the emotional level, Sheila Tobias and others have helped women achieve in mathematics at rates equal to, and surpassing, those of men.

But the divided life is not just an academic dilemma, it's a human dilemma. We work within institutions like schools, businesses, and civic society, because they provide us with opportunities that we value. But the claims those institutions make on us are sometimes at odds with our hearts—for example, the demand for loyalty to the corporation, right or wrong, can conflict with the inward imperative to speak truth. That tension can be creative, up to a point. But it becomes pathological when the heart becomes a wholly owned subsidiary of the organization, when we internalize organizational logic and allow it to overwhelm the logic of our own lives.

At a certain juncture, some people find they must choose between allowing selfhood to die or claiming their identity and integrity. What I mean by divided-no-more is living on the outside the truth you know on the inside.

INTERVIEWER: What happens to people's lives when they make that choice, to live "divided-no-more"?

PALMER: Let me tell you a story about two teachers, a story I tell in *The Courage to Teach*.

Alan and Eric were born into different families of skilled rural craftspeople. Each grew skilled in working with his hands and developed a sense of pride in their respective crafts. Both also excelled in school and became the first in their families to go to college, eventually earning doctorates and choosing academic careers.

Here their paths diverged. Eric, who attended an elite private college, suffered culture shock and was always insecure with fellow students and later with academic colleagues. He learned to speak and act like an intellectual, but he always felt fraudulent. This insecurity didn't draw Eric into self-reflection; instead, he bullied his way through his professional life, made pronouncements rather than probes, listened for weaknesses rather than strengths in what other people said. In his classroom, Eric was critical and judgmental, quick to put down "stupid questions," adept at using trick questions of his own, and merciless in mocking wrong answers.

Alan's is a different story. He attended a land-grant university where many students had backgrounds much like his own. He was not driven to hide his gift, but was able to honor and transform it by turning it toward his work in academia. Watching Alan teach, you felt that you were watching a craftsman at work. In his lectures, every move Alan made was informed by attention to detail and respect for the materials at hand. Beyond the classroom, students knew that Alan would extend himself with great generosity to any of them who wanted to become his apprentice.

Alan taught from an undivided self—an integral state of being in which every major thread of one's life experience is honored, creating a weave of coherence and strength. Such a self is able to make the outward connections on which good teaching depends.

INTERVIEWER: There's another dimension implicit here. I gather that you support teachers bringing their learnings from their spiritual life into the classroom.

PALMER: Yes, in fact, I'd put it even more strongly than that. I don't see how a teacher or any human being can fail to bring their spirituality into whatever it is they're doing. And by that I don't mean the content of one's religious belief. I mean the way we deal with fundamental questions like "What am I doing here?" and "Does my life have a meaning?" and "Does that meaning depend on how successful I am in whatever I'm doing?" and "What about the fact that I'm going to die one day?"

These are the same questions that our students have. We need to find ways to support our students in asking these questions. I'm not saying we need to give them the answers. These are questions that you wrap your life around. As the poet Rainer Maria Rilke said, you live these questions and don't try to get formulaic answers to them. They're too important for that.

INTERVIEWER: There are those who feel that schools ought to make sure that young people get "correct" answers to those questions.

One of the traditions that many people feel very strongly about is the separation of church and schooling or church and state.

PALMER: I absolutely believe in the separation of church and state. As a Quaker, I come from a history of people who were persecuted, imprisoned, even executed by folks who found our religious beliefs nonconforming with the truth they knew absolutely.

But I think that the surest way to encourage religious fascism is to sweep questions of meaning under the rug; pretend that either they don't exist or that they aren't important, rather than to hold these questions in a way that illuminates them and helps young people learn to live them more and more deeply.

INTERVIEWER: Have you seen that done successfully?

PALMER: I was teaching, not too long ago, at a college in Appalachia where the students came from very fundamentalist religious backgrounds. In the middle of the year, the Dalai Lama visited the college. There was a group of students who protested this visit; from their point of view, the Dalai Lama was the Antichrist.

One of these students started talking in class about what a terrible thing it was that the Tibetan Buddhists hold certain beliefs about the Dalai Lama. He said he felt it was especially ridiculous that the Tibetans went out and found a young child, somehow magically decided that he was the one they were seeking, and then raised him up to his current status.

I said to him, "Like you, I'm a Christian, and what I need to do is to explore with you the fact that our own faith tradition has a very similar belief. In fact, we believe that we identified Jesus when he was an infant, younger even than the boy that became the Dalai Lama."

Well, that opened up a dialogue about some very basic questions, such as how people discern reality. I framed this as an open question—I didn't put [that student] down for putting down someone else, but simply held up as a matter of wonder that around the world, we look at babies and young children and we say that they have something of truth that we need and want to nurture into larger life. So what could have been a shoot-out became a genuine conversation. Months later he thanked me and said that he'd never stopped thinking about this conversation.

INTERVIEWER: Talking to people with values so different from our own can be very scary. How do you overcome your own fear and that of your students?

PALMER: The answer is not to avoid situations where you feel fearful; the more you try to ignore fear or to sweep it under the rug, the stronger it becomes. There's a curious alchemy in the spiritual life—when I acknowledge and embrace those parts of myself that are most difficult, I find they have less power over me or that the power somehow starts working for me rather than against me.

INTERVIEWER: We've been talking so far mainly about the inner work of being divided-no-more—learning to be true to ourselves, and getting beyond our fears. What about the implications for society? What happens on a larger scale when people decide they will no longer live divided lives?

PALMER: In political/social terms, I call this the Rosa Parks decision. She essentially said, "I'm no longer going to behave on the outside as if I were less than the full person I know myself to be on the inside."

How do people find the courage to bring inner convictions into harmony with outer acts, knowing the risks involved? I think in Rosa Parks's story there's a clue. When the police came to Rosa Parks on the bus and informed her that they would have to put her in jail if she did not move, she replied, "You may do that." It was a very polite way of saying, "How could your jail begin to compare with the jail I have had myself in all these years by collaborating with this racist system?"

When you realize that you can no longer collaborate in something that violates your own integrity, your understanding of punishment is suddenly transformed.

INTERVIEWER: How does this individual act set the stage for a larger shift in society?

PALMER: In the second stage of a movement, people who have chosen the undivided life but still feel shaky about it come together in "communities of congruence." The first purpose of these communities is mutual reassurance; people help each other to understand that the "normal" behavior expected by the institutions they are part of can be crazy, but that seeking integrity is always sane. In the movement sparked by Rosa Parks, the black churches provided gathering places for people who needed to know that they were not alone in choosing an integral life.

These communities are also places where people begin to develop the language to explain their vision—and that language provides the strength they will need in the rough-and-tumble world of the public realm, which is where a movement goes into the third stage.

As a movement goes public, the identity and integrity of its participants are tested against the great diversity of values and visions at work in the public arena. Paradoxically, although we must stay close to our own integrity in this complex field of forces, we must also risk opening ourselves to conflicting influences, because in that way both the movement and our integrity can grow.

In the final stage, the movement returns to alter the logic of the organizations from which it first sprang. Movements have this power when people decide that the institution's punishments are irrelevant and develop an alternative system of rewards. In the first stage, the rewards involve learning more about one's identity. In Stage 2, the reward comes from being in community. In Stage 3, the reward comes in living a more expansive public life. In Stage 4, people are clear that no reward anyone offers them could be greater than the way they reward themselves by living their own truth. As this happens, institutions often awaken to the need for change, lest the action go elsewhere and they become irrelevant to people's lives.

INTERVIEWER: That's a powerful analysis of social movements. I guess I don't normally think of teachers as social change activists.

PALMER: I am a teacher at heart, and I am not naturally drawn to political activism. But I've found that there is no essential conflict between loving to teach and working to reform education. An authentic movement is not a play for power—it is teaching and learning writ large. Now the world becomes our classroom, and the potential to teach and learn is found everywhere. We need only be in the world as our true selves, with open hearts and minds.

LINDA LANTIERI

A Vision of Schools with Spirit

> Education should be a source of nurturance for the
> spirit as well as a means of reaching understanding.
>
> —Linda Darling-Hammond

*W*hen we open the discussion of nurturing children's and teachers' spiritual lives, it's important to say exactly what we are talking about. Although connected to moral development and ethical principles, nurturing the spiritual is neither. Morality is about right and wrong, and often causes judgment and separation between people and groups of people with different cultural values. The word "spiritual" often conjures up religious dogma, a set of beliefs and practices one might have. Religion can indeed be an expression of one's spiritual nature, but many people nurture the spiritual dimension of their lives without adhering to a specific religion. The definition of "spiritual" that we are exploring in this book encompasses a realm of human life that is nonjudgmental and integrated. It is about belonging and connectedness, meaning and purpose. Spiritual experience cannot be taught. But it can be uncovered, evoked, found, and recovered.

Humans have the capacity for creativity, for love, for meaning and purpose, for wisdom, beauty, and justice. All these are aspects of our spiritual lives. When they are evoked, the experience is often subjective and intensely "real." Apollo 14 astronaut Captain Edgar Mitchell describes it this way:

On February 9, 1971, when I went to the moon, I was as pragmatic a test pilot, engineer and scientist as any of my colleagues. But when I saw the planet Earth floating in the vastness of space . . . the presence of divinity became almost palpable and I knew that life in the universe was not just an accident based on random processes. It was a knowledge gained through subjective awareness, but it was—and still is—every bit as real as the objective data upon which the navigational program was based.[1]

Spiritual experience can be described as the conscious recognition of a connection that goes beyond our own minds or emotions. It's the kind of experience that sometimes leaves us without words to describe it—in my own case, I think of walking through the woods in Alaska, coming face to face with a moose and her calf, and instinctively communicating that I wasn't going to harm them.

Most of us have experienced this essence of our human spirit in powerful encounters with nature—from glorious sunsets to the sound of the ocean. Or we may have been deeply moved by a piece of music or by a certain soul-to-soul flow between ourselves and someone else that lifts us beyond the mundane. Swiss psychologist Carl Jung used the term "synchronicity" to describe "meaningful coincidences" that are so timely that they seem beyond chance. If we have engaged with intensity in a sport or the martial arts, we may have experienced the "high" of a sensory experience that brings a natural spiritual release. And a social issue can arouse our passions and connect us to a group consciousness that touches the divine within us.

What would it mean to nurture these experiences in schools in more intentional ways so that our classrooms could be places that facilitate spiritual growth? What would it be like if soul were more present in our schools? In the "schools of spirit" that I envision, the following would be true.

- The uniqueness and inherent value of every individual would be honored, and education would be seen as a lifelong process.
- Students and teachers alike would be engaged in inquiry, exploring and learning about what has heart and meaning for themselves. Different ways of knowing would be respected— those we could test for and others too subjective to be measured.

- School leaders would shift from a centralized concept of power to approaches that help individuals and groups to self-organize.
- We would be less concerned with the "school spirit" that comes from winning a football game and more concerned with the spirit of collaboration and partnership, and with an appreciation of diversity within the school community.
- We would acknowledge our interconnectedness, with one another and with all of life, by a commitment to ecological principles, environmental limits, and social responsibility.
- We would enlarge our ability to put to use our gifts of intuition, imagination, and creativity.
- We would value personal change as a vehicle for systemic change and social justice.
- There would be places and time for silence and stillness, to help us face the chaos and complexity of school life yet stay in touch with inner truth and the web of interconnectedness.
- We would pay as much attention to whether a student knows his or her unique purpose in life as we do to his or her SAT scores.

In short, I believe we need to see schools as active and alive organisms that place the highest value on self-knowledge, healthy interpersonal relationships, and building community. These goals are not incompatible with the pursuit of academic excellence—indeed, they foster it—but without care, respect, and kindness, what purpose does intellectual competence serve?

Recently the Resolving Conflict Creatively Program released one of the largest scientific evaluations of a school-based social and emotional learning program ever completed. The results supported the conclusion that two years of teaching five thousand young people concrete skills in managing their emotions and resolving conflict actually interrupted the developmental pathways that could otherwise lead to violence and aggression.[2] When I had the privilege of being on a panel with Archbishop Desmond Tutu soon after the presentation of this report at an international Appeal for Peace conference at The Hague, he smiled when he heard of the study's results. "By the looks of things," he said, "we could be in deep trouble. Imagine these peacemaking skills being incorporated throughout a child's entire education. I'm not sure we would have enough people in the world who would be willing to kill or be killed in wars or who would want a job that has the power to press the button that could cause a nuclear holocaust."[3]

The contributors to *Schools with Spirit* inspire us to help each child know that he or she matters. They ask us to pursue those teachable moments that will outlast our test scores. They encourage us not to miss opportunities to address life's deepest questions because of fear of being "off task" or venturing into a realm that is forbidden in public schools. They remind us that what we do about welcoming the inner life into our classrooms will matter.

Why We Need Schools with Spirit

As we step into the new millennium, we are holding in our individual and collective hands the opportunity to use our civilization's new knowledge and advances for unbearable evil, devastation, and moral breakdown—or for goodness, transformation, and hope. The choices we make today regarding how we nurture our children's development will have critical implications for generations to come. Even as we make huge advances in the world of technology and our understanding of the brain, in this country we are struggling to rescue generations of young people who are growing up without the supports they need to feel valued and to participate in community. Although Yale psychiatrist James Comer tells us that "we are doing the least harm to the most privileged," according to the Annie E. Casey Foundation's "Kids Count" for 1999, 21 percent of American children still live in poverty and "are growing up with a collection of risk factors that are profoundly unsettling."[4]

Too many young people experience mental health and adjustment difficulties, and our schools don't have the resources to provide appropriate help and attention. It is estimated that one out of five nine- to seventeen-year-olds has a diagnosable mental disorder.[5] The fact is that an increasing number of children are entering schools in crisis—unprepared cognitively and emotionally to learn. Educators confront the challenge of higher public expectations and diminishing internal resources to do their jobs well.

This complex set of social conditions tries the best of us who work in public education. Instead of fostering meaningful discourse, tolerance of divergent thinking, and the opportunity to get to know ourselves and each other, most public schools today look more like what social psychologist Alfie Kohn calls "giant test prep centers." In most, the deeper questions of life have been put on the back burner. As educators we are somewhat aware of this void, yet we are not sure what to do about it. Many of us recognize that a "one size fits all" standardized system of education may have been useful during the industrial age, but will not be adequate to prepare our children for living together in the new millennium.

In my work with teachers, principals, and parents, I've asked hundreds of groups in the United States and other countries, If you could go to bed tonight and wake up in the morning with the power to ensure that you could teach one thing to all the children of the world, what would it be?

The responses are similar no matter where I am or whom I ask: that children feel loved; that they know they have a purpose; that they learn tolerance and compassion; that they have a sense of their interconnectedness with other people and with the natural world. The tragedy is that no present system of public education in our country attends consciously and systematically to that which we clearly feel matters most. *Schools with Spirit* is about making these wishes a reality.

In a recent survey of 272 global thinkers from around the world, five shared values emerged: compassion, honesty, fairness, responsibility, and respect.[6] These values seem to be so universal that it appears that they are agreed upon regardless of one's religious or spiritual perspective. When the American Association of School Administrators asked fifty education leaders a similar question—What would students need to know and be able to do and what behaviors would they need to thrive during the next century?—civility and ethical behavior were on the list along with math and science.[7] So we seem to agree on some of the fundamental tasks of education, and that they extend beyond helping young people stay out of trouble and achieve academic competence. However, we have not yet outlined the steps needed to strengthen these shared values. What role can our schools play in shifting our strategies to welcome a more intentional development of the emotional, social, and spiritual domains of our students' lives?

The current school reform movement has often made use of "visioning" workshops, in which school personnel go through carefully thought-out steps to produce a mission statement for their school, upon which future changes are then based. I remember being involved in such a process myself a few years ago, as our own organization created a five-year strategic plan. What I was struck by was that although we seemed to reach clarity, consensus, and commitment to our basic future direction, we didn't pay enough attention to our inner world. For my part, what mattered most to me and what was at the core of my being didn't get mentioned in our strategic plan, and upon reflection I believe that there were other people in our organization who felt a similar dissatisfaction. In schools, the current strategic planning process often suppresses and distorts inner vision in favor of looking at existing trends and financial goals. When this happens, leaders and staff are not able to bring their wholehearted energy and commitment to the task at hand. Some would say that when this incongruence exists, it's time to look for another job. But this assumes that neither the person nor the organization is growing and changing. How can an organization or a school go off in a direction that does not have heart and meaning at its core? And of course the reverse is true as well. Leadership alone cannot pursue a direction that the rest of the organization is not ready for. In schools, administrators and teachers must link up their sense of mission with personal vision, spirit, and vitality. It is the genuine and spontaneous energy of our inner lives that gives us the ability to translate our vision into concrete steps and to implement it.

Issues of Church and State

The movement to welcome children's and teachers' inner lives into our classrooms comes at a time when our society is becoming more and more open to matters of the spirit. People from all walks of life are regularly discussing spirituality and the inner life. Many feel that the survival of the human race depends on waking up to this dimension in a deeper way. A 1998 Gallup poll reported that 82 percent of those surveyed felt that spiritual growth was a very important part of their lives.[8] Since 1993, the sale of spiritually oriented books has increased eight-fold. And those who see spiritual growth as an important part of their lives are part of mainstream culture—only 6 percent of them consider themselves "new age."[9] Another national survey reports that religion and spirituality are among the most important values for seven out of ten Americans. Although interest in these matters is clearly widespread, our schools still do not reflect this concern.[10]

For most of us working in schools, it may be helpful to understand more about the parameters of the First Amendment, which many of us feel limits our freedom to discuss spiritual concerns in the classroom. There is much confusion about what the First Amendment tells us we can and cannot do. Knowing what the law actually says can shed light on doing work in this area.[11] The Constitution recognizes religious faith as a fundamental right of the individual, superseding government intervention. This means that the government cannot do anything to promote religious faith, but the government cannot do anything to undermine it either. The Supreme Court clearly supports the study of religion, as well as the inclusion of religion in the curriculum in historical and cultural contexts. Teachers are encouraged not to advocate a particular point of view, but to accept the expression of young people's religious views as germane to an open discussion, a homework assignment, or any other academic project.

The right of religious expression in schools does not include the right to have a "captive audience listen or to compel other students to participate," but it does allow individual students to pray, read scripture, discuss their faith, and even invite others to join their own particular religious group, as long as this is not coercive or disruptive to others. Although school officials may not organize religious activities, including prayer, they may lead a group in a moment of silence. Schools need to be places that neither inculcate nor inhibit religion. Religious conviction should be treated with fairness and respect.

The use of music, art, drama, and literature with religious themes is also permissible if it serves an educational curriculum goal, as long as this does not become a vehicle to promote a particular religious belief. You can study the significance of a religious holiday or present school concerts of sacred music. At the secondary school level, students may also form religious clubs wherever other non-curriculum-related clubs are allowed, and these groups must have the same freedom to use school facilities and media, as well as to distribute literature of a religious nature. It is useful to see how much leeway our courts have given schools in this realm—much more than many educators in public schools have come to believe they have.

My understanding of the body of law surrounding the interpretation of the First Amendment is that it doesn't set guidelines for the kind of nurturing of the spiritual dimension that this book is addressing. What guidelines we do have about the subject are still based on the quite narrow assumption that anything spiritual equals religion. However, it's important to understand how broad the right of even specifically "religious" expression in schools is.

Risk and Resilience

When we look carefully at the literature on "resilience"—those capacities that foster healthy development—we find an attempt to co-ordinate the social, emotional, moral, physical, and cognitive development of young people.[12] Researchers and practitioners who focus on resiliency offer us a model of looking at young people's lives from a strength-based perspective. They go beyond the identification of "risk factors" such as poverty and social dislocation to the study of how young people's strengths and capabilities can be developed in order to protect them from the potential harm that those risk factors represent. This body of research has direct relevance for our concerns about the nurturing of the inner lives of young people. For example, the Search Institute studied over 100,000 sixth through twelfth graders in 213 towns and cities in the United States in order to identify the "building blocks of healthy development" that assist young people in choosing positive paths, making wise decisions, and growing up to be caring and responsible adults. Their research identified forty positive experiences or qualities, called "developmental assets," which have a significant positive influence on young people's lives.

According to the Search Institute, the presence of these "assets" in young people's lives serves to protect them from engaging in problem behaviors and harmful and unhealthy choices ranging from alcohol and drug abuse to depression and attempted suicide. Several of them pertain to what I would describe as young people's inner lives. In the list below, the Search Institute's designation for each is followed by its operational criteria regarding that experience or quality.

- *Service to others*—serves in the community one hour or more per week
- *Religious community*—spends one or more hours per week in activities in a religious institution
- *Creative activities*—spends three to four hours per week in lessons or practice in music, theater, or the arts
- *Caring*—places high value on helping others
- *Integrity*—acts on convictions and stands up for his or her beliefs
- *Honesty*—tells the truth even when it's not easy
- *Personal power*—has control over "things that happen to me"
- *Sense of purpose*—reports that "my life has a purpose"
- *Positive view of personal future*—is optimistic about his or her personal future

This kind of research points to some of the ways in which our educational institutions can contribute to positive resilient outcomes for youth. The facilitation of these protective factors is important for both adults and young people, and clearly it involves developing inner strengths that can serve to prevent or repair harm.

Many young people today are cut off from an understanding of their lives as having a "higher purpose"—or any purpose at all. Many have trouble even imagining what their future will look like. Psychiatrist James Garbarino, author of *Lost Boys,* calls this "terminal thinking," which he warns can undermine young people's motivation to contribute to their community and invest in their present life circumstances. He also discusses what he calls "juvenile vigilantism," speaking of violent boys who have lost confidence in the ability of adults to protect and care for them and so join gangs in order to feel a little safer rather than not safe at all.[13]

The kind of spiritual development we are advocating is not about allowing schools to display the Ten Commandments in their classrooms. We are talking about the kinds of approaches that encourage a commitment to matters of the heart and spirit that are among the positive building blocks of healthy development.

The Development of Social and Emotional Competencies

Another trend in educational theory that has paved the way for nurturing children's spirits in schools is the social and emotional learning movement popularized by the best-selling book *Emotional Intelligence,* by social psychologist Daniel Goleman (1995).[14] Goleman has contributed much to our thinking about the need to nurture the social and emotional lives of children, by summarizing research from the fields of neuroscience and cognitive psychology that identifies EQ—emotional intelligence—as being as important as IQ in terms of children's healthy development and future life success. He writes,

> One of psychology's open secrets is the relative inability of grades, IQ, or SAT scores, despite their popular mystiques, to predict unerringly who will succeed in life. . . . There are widespread exceptions to the rule that IQ predicts success—many (or more) exceptions than cases that fit the rule. At best IQ contributes about 20 percent to the factors that determine life success, which leaves 80 percent to other forces.

Goleman's work and the term "emotional intelligence" have come into wider use as a result of millions of readers worldwide who now have been exposed to the idea that children's social and emotional development must be attended to first in any educational framework if we are to produce healthy citizens.

In fact, it was Howard Gardner, with his earlier "multiple intelligences" model, who paved the way for expanding our concept of intelligence. The "personal intelligences" he outlined included intrapersonal intelligence, which involves knowing and managing one's own feelings, and interpersonal intelligence, which is the ability to understand and get along with others. Gardner has since considered the addition of three new intelligences to the list. They include a naturalist intelligence, a spiritual intelligence, and an existential intelligence. While the evidence to support the inclusion of each is varied, Gardner's ideas have a lot to do with the kind of abilities or capacities that schools with spirit would promote.[15]

Goleman helped educators make the important link between one's emotional intelligence as a basic requirement for the effective use of one's IQ—that is, our cognitive skills and knowledge.[16] He made the connection between our feelings and our thinking more explicit, by pointing out how the brain's emotional and executive areas are interconnected physiologically, especially as these areas relate to teaching and learning. The prefrontal lobes of the brain, which control emotional impulses, are also where working memory resides and all learning takes place. But working memory has a limited attention capacity. Goleman's summary of recent neuroscientific research made us aware that when chronic anxiety, anger, or upset feelings are intruding on children's thoughts, less room is available in working memory to process what they are trying to learn. This implies that at least in part academic success depends on a student's ability to maintain positive social interactions. As a result of Goleman's work, schools across the country began helping children strengthen their EQ by equipping them with concrete skills for identifying and managing their emotions, communicating effectively, and resolving conflicts nonviolently. These skills help children to make good decisions, to be more empathetic, and to be optimistic in the face of setbacks.

Many school systems across the country have used the frameworks developed by social scientists to bring together under one umbrella various different efforts for preventing "risky" behavior among young people, from alcohol and drug use to premature sexual activity. This approach acknowledges that the development of social and emotional skills is a critical factor in school-based prevention efforts, and it calls for an integration of the cognitive and affective domains because the academic and personal success of students will depend on it.

Spiritual Intelligence

In the late 1990s, Danah Zohar, a visiting fellow at Oxford University, and Ian Marshall, a practicing psychiatrist, did for spiritual intelligence what Daniel Goleman did for emotional intelligence.[17] They brought together an array of recent research that showed evidence that there is an "ultimate intelligence based on a third neural system in the brain"—a spiritual intelligence.

Spiritual intelligence, or SQ, as Zohar and Marshall call it, is "the intelligence with which we address and solve problems of meaning and value, the intelligence with which we can place our actions and our lives in a wider, richer meaning-giving context. It is the intelligence with which we can assess that one course of action or one life path is more meaningful than another." They point out that neither IQ nor EQ can fully explain the complexity of human intelligence or the richness of the human soul. Computers have high IQs; animals can be highly sensitive to their owner's moods. The "why" questions—asking how things could be better or different—and the ability to envision unrealized possibilities or to wrestle with questions of good and evil are all in the realm of SQ, according to Zohar and Marshall. They call spiritual intelligence the ultimate intelligence because it is the necessary foundation for the effective functioning of the other intelligences and because it has a transformative power. The distinction they make between EQ and SQ is the following:

> My emotional intelligence allows me to judge what situation I am in and then behave appropriately within it. This is working *within* the boundaries of the situation, allowing the situation to guide *me*. But my spiritual intelligence allows me to ask if I want to be in this particular situation in the first place. Would I rather change the situation, creating a better one? This is working *with* the boundaries of the situation, allowing me to guide the situation.

Zohar and Marshall's work attempts to distill what scientific evidence we do have concerning this realm of experience, even though they are the first to admit that existing science is not well equipped to study something like meaning and its role in our lives. However, as they point out, a great deal of data does exist which could be helpful as supportive evidence for the need to more intentionally include the development of this intelligence in our classrooms. They also outline some useful competencies, skills, or qualities of a spiritually intelligent person. They are the following:

- *A high degree of self-awareness*—knowing who we are, what our strengths and limits are, what we live for
- *The capacity to be inspired by vision and values*—a caring that transcends self-interest; having a sense of service
- *The ability to face and use suffering and transcend pain*—learn-

ing from mistakes, our own and those of others; acknowledging our weaknesses and cultivating our strengths

- *A holistic worldview*—an ability to see connections between diverse things and see the bigger picture
- *An appreciation of diversity*—being grateful for differences that challenge our assumptions and values and make us grow
- *Being "field independent"*—possessing the capacity to stand against the crowd or work against convention
- *Spontaneity*—the ability to be flexible and actively adaptive
- *A marked tendency to ask "why" or "what" questions and seek "fundamental" answers*
- *Compassion*—a reluctance to cause unnecessary harm

Spirituality in Young Children

British researchers David Hay and Rebecca Nye, coauthors of the book *The Spirit of the Child,* have done research on the lives of young children that suggests that spiritual awareness and expression may be a natural predisposition, a biological reality.[18] In fact, Nye and Hay see spirituality as a given of the human condition and a byproduct of evolution. Among the areas of childhood experience they link to the spiritual dimension are the following:

Awareness of the "here-and-now" as opposed to dwelling in the past or future; this is crucial to the practices of prayer, meditation, and contemplation

Awareness of "mystery" of those aspects of the human experience that can't be explained easily

Awareness of value, that is, an intensity of feeling about "what we most value"

To investigate such elusive concepts, Hay and Nye asked children to respond to a series of photographs depicting subjects such as a girl gazing into a fire, a boy looking out at the stars, a girl crying as she looks at her dead pet gerbil. Their first and most important finding was that although they themselves avoided prompting for religious concepts, they did not come across a single child without a sense of spirituality, even though very few in their study came from religious homes. Indeed, the majority of the children in their sample had very limited religious vocabularies and instead used the language of fairy tales or science fiction to express what Hay and Nye call "relational consciousness," that is, an intense awareness of relatedness—to God, to nature, to other people, or to self.

Clearly, such a predisposition connects closely to ethical and moral behavior. It helps us begin to make the link between damage to oneself and damage to others, care for oneself and care for others. Acknowledging these connections between social and moral development and the implications of research on the deeper implication of spiritual awareness in young children can help us begin the dialogue about what the content of a spiritual curriculum might include.

NANCY CARLSSON-PAIGE

Nurturing Meaningful Connections with Young Children

CELÍN: Does Mama ever cry?
MAMI: Yes, she does. Everyone cries sometime.
CELÍN: Not dead people.
MAMI: Nope, they don't have any more tears.
CELÍN: And they can't move, so their spirits come out and play.

*C*elín will soon be going to kindergarten. She often surprises her mother with the things she says, especially when they relate to spiritual matters. But when Celín gets to school, she will probably figure out quickly that these spiritual ideas which she finds so interesting belong to a part of her experience that she should not mention in school.

From their first days of life, children are trying to make sense of things. They actively engage with the world around them, exploring, manipulating, interacting with everything and everyone within reach. Just watching a baby lay a piece of string on top of a shoe as if it were a shoelace or a toddler cover up a stuffed animal at bedtime reminds us that children's actions are full of purpose. These explorations and experiments involve a child's thoughts and feelings as one inseparable whole; minds and hearts work together effortlessly in the early years as children actively create meaning from their experience.

The mounting body of literature known to many educators today as constructivist education is united by the central idea that children actively *construct* meaning for themselves. These meanings, unique to each child, are embedded in family and culture and built over time. Because of this, a basic aim of education should be to begin with children's personal meanings as the foundation on which to build new learning. But in order to do so, those of us who work with young children may need to open our lenses more widely, let go of some of our pre-set ideas, and be willing and able to see what children put before us.

Losing Oneself in School

When children enter school, they bring with them their natural capacity for making meaning. But for many children, arriving at school means leaving some of themselves behind. Much of school curriculum requires children to meet the demands of tasks that do not build on their previous understanding of the world, and all too often the emphasis on right answers begins to separate children from themselves.

A student teacher assigned to an early childhood classroom wrote this in the journal she kept for her graduate school seminar:[1]

> Jasper sat with the worksheet page on two-place addition in front of him. He was supposed to add 35 and 23 in the first problem. I came over and saw that he was trying to add the numbers horizontally instead of vertically! He didn't understand at all what he was doing. I've done Piagetian number tasks with Jasper and I know he doesn't even conserve number yet![2] This assignment can't make any sense to him. He needs to be working on pre-number concepts with manipulatives. He was getting so frustrated and upset. He said to me, "I think I'm gonna cry. Do I go down? Go down, right? I don't know what to do." I tried to help him even though I knew this was all wrong. He got more and more upset so I finally suggested he stop. The head teacher came over and said, "If he was made to do it through recess, you'd see how quickly he'd learn it."

Unfortunately, school experiences like Jasper's are not uncommon. When children are expected to complete tasks that are not geared to their understanding, they become confused, begin to feel inadequate, begin to doubt their own ability to make sense.

In addition, a focus on "the basics" in schools forces a large part of children's experience aside, especially the social, emotional, and spiritual dimensions of their lives. Howard Gardner's theory of multiple intelligences, first put forth in the early 1980s,[3] has expanded our understanding of the ways in which we make sense, but it is still the linguistic and logical/mathematical intelligences that dominate our schools. Children's capacities for meaning making through drawing, drama, music, social exchange, and inner exploration are being given less and less room in the curriculum.

But it is the spiritual dimension of children's lives more than any other that has been excluded from school life. Concerns about the separation of church and state have led to schools that compartmentalize minds, hearts, and souls. These areas of experience are not separate for young children, though they learn quickly to draw lines between them once they get to school.

In considering the possibility of a spiritual or existential intelligence, Gardner has recently written of the human capacity to engage with transcendental concerns. As an educator who has studied young children for many years, I am interested in how this capacity first shows itself in children. My own two sons began asking questions about God by the age of five (ours was a secular household); each evolved his own theories about the nature of life and things beyond himself and revised these again and again throughout childhood.

Writers Robert Coles and Thomas Armstrong have each documented the rich and varied spiritual lives of children of various religious and secular backgrounds.[4] Both comment that Western psychology, rooted in the scientific and secular, has neglected children's inner lives: we cannot see what we have no maps for interpreting.

Many parents from both religious and secular backgrounds have told me stories of how their children weave spiritual ideas into the meanings they make. Here is Celín's mother reporting on a conversation with Celín at age four:

> Celín has gotten a little abrasion on the inside of her wrist. It smarts, and we have put a bandaid on it, but she is still a little weepy. I am holding her in my lap telling her all the reasons that I love her. "Because you are smart, sweet, gentle, strong. You do a spectacular monkey, you're funny, creative . . . "
> CELÍN: Funny?
> MAMI: Yes, you are very funny and you make me laugh.
> CELÍN: But I hurt myself.
> MAMI: Yes, I know. But you know what? Everybody hurts themselves once in a while.
> CELÍN: Not God?

MAMI: No, not God.
CELÍN: But God is everywhere.
MAMI: Yes, God is everywhere.
CELÍN: Even in you and me.
MAMI: Yes.
CELÍN: Well then if God is in me, God is hurt.[5]

While conversations such as this one seem to be fairly common for parents and their children, they are not so common among teachers and students. In my twenty-five years in classrooms, I have not heard one child voice spiritual ideas in a school discussion. The message that such ideas are taboo at school must be learned very early.

In her discussion of the separation of church and state, Rachael Kessler makes the important distinction between teachers espousing their beliefs and children expressing theirs.[6] What has happened as teachers try to keep religion out of school, she says, is the suppression of students' exploration of their own beliefs, longings, and search for spiritual meaning.

Children's spiritual questions and ideas can come to school if teachers can find ways to let them in. Teachers can listen for these ideas and accept them openly. They can facilitate discussions among children who are expressing spiritually based ideas without imposing their own views.

The need for schools to become communities that embrace the wholeness of the human experience is greater now than ever before. But the current standards-driven educational climate has edged out multiple ways of seeing and being and has driven an even bigger wedge between curriculum expectations and children's views of the world. Ironically, this is occurring at the same time that alienated young people are bringing guns to school and shooting classmates. This is a time when the inner lives, deeper selves, and spiritual longings of students are crying out for educators' attention.

A Culture That Divides

In a country where 1 percent of the population holds 48 percent of the wealth and where 20 percent of children live below the poverty line, stress of all kinds falls unevenly and unfairly onto children. A host of risk factors such as violence, poverty, racism, and poor health add up to what James Garbarino calls a "socially toxic environment" for many children.[7]

These risk factors are compounded by the negative effects of a media culture that uses aggressive marketing campaigns aimed at children. This all-pervasive influence affects virtually every child in the country long before his or her arrival at school. The children with the most stress in their lives are the most vulnerable to these influences, but all children feel their impact.

I first began to realize how significantly media culture was affecting young children in the mid-1980s, when teachers began telling me that children's play was changing and that they were concerned about it. This was just after the broadcasting industry had been deregulated under the Reagan administration, which opened the floodgates for big business to market TV-linked toys and products to children, a practice prohibited before that time by the Federal Communications Commission. The onslaught of shows, products, and toys linked together around a single theme began to saturate children's worlds with commercialized images, especially with images of violence. Large numbers of teachers began to describe how children were imitating TV scripts in their play and acting out the violence they had seen instead of inventing their own stories. These teachers were concerned that the deep meanings that young children construct when their play flows from their own needs and experience were being replaced at least in part by content seen on the screen.

Teachers know that children use play as a central vehicle for reordering their experience and making meaning of it. As the developmental psychologist Jean Piaget observed decades ago,[8] children's active invention and reinvention of ideas, which often occurs in play, is the road to genuine understanding. If a young child gets accidentally knocked over by a huge barking dog, for instance, she will create a host of ways to reenact the experience until she has made sense of it to her satisfaction. She might act out the scene over and over with toy animals, or draw pictures of the scary dog, or tell a story that sounds something like what happened mixed in with elements from her own imagination. This process of active meaning making goes on for young children constantly and is the core means by which they make sense of everything; through it children continually create a sense of equilibrium with their own experience, making it possible to integrate new experiences with those of the past.

Since those early observations by teachers about the media culture's influence on children, things have only gotten worse. Today media cross-feeding has intensified as videos, computer games, Hollywood movies, and fast-food chains have joined in the marketing mix. Children spend almost forty hours a week consuming this media output outside of school, much of it violent.[9] The hours spent alone in front of a screen rob children of vital social lessons they need to be learning from spontaneous play with their peers. The lost hours of positive learning with friends and classmates are replaced by interactions with media messages that are often deeply antisocial. By the end of elementary school, the average child will have witnessed 8,000 murders and 100,000 other acts of violence on television.[10] What teachers saw early on is now conclusively supported by research: viewing entertainment violence leads to increases in aggressive behavior and attitudes in children and desensitizes them to violence.[11]

Young children are easily desensitized to violence because they can't make sense of it. They are drawn to the action and excitement without understanding its negative effects. They develop an appetite for violence before ever understanding that in real life it's not fun and it hurts.

Because of the influence of this kind of popular culture in children's lives, the meaning-making efforts of many children are undermined long before they ever get to school. These cultural forces taken together tend to separate children from themselves and from one another; they lead to the social, emotional, and spiritual disconnection that many young people feel today.

Schools cannot possibly solve the problems created by societal influences of this magnitude, but we can do a great deal to help children connect meaningfully to themselves and to others in school. Children need to come to school with all of their feelings, all of their ideas, all of their questions; they need teachers who can reach *toward* them and the fullness of who they are, who can build new ideas onto the meanings children have made; they need help learning about their own inner feelings and the feelings of others; and they need to experience the joys and struggles of being part of a group.

What we are seeing currently in education is a general trend in the opposite direction of fulfilling these needs. Nevertheless, many teachers continue to find ways to nurture the growth of the whole child, to open up channels for deep connection among children. What do classrooms that nurture this kind of wholeness look like?

Inviting the Whole Child In

Kirsten's kindergarten classroom is in an urban public school.[12] Kirsten holds daily class meetings where children are free to talk about their school work and their lives. She listens intently for the meanings behind what children say.

One day at class meeting a boy named Carlos asked to speak and began to talk about something that troubled him deeply.

Here's how Kirsten tells what happened:

> Carlos asked if he could share something with our class at sharing time. He said that his parents were fighting over the weekend and it made him feel scared. Then he said, "I'm ready for questions and comments." One of the students told him they were sorry that had happened. Another student wanted to know if they were fighting with words or with their bodies. Carlos told him that it was a fight with words, but it was really loud and lasted for a long time. He felt really scared because he wasn't sure what to do. The same student wondered if they fought a lot, and Carlos told him that they didn't, which was why he was so scared. When all of the questions were finished, we asked Carlos what we could do to make him feel a little bit better. He thought we could send him lots of love and hugs (something that our class sends to each other when we are feeling sad or vulnerable).
>
> During lunch and nap time, my student teacher and I talked a lot about this because Carlos had obviously been very upset, and the children had a lot to say. We talked about our own feelings when we heard arguments between family members as children. We decided to focus afternoon work time on this idea: What happens when you hear or see other people fight? How do you feel? We centered this in four areas of the classroom:
>
> *Writing:* In the middle of the table we wrote: "When I see people fight, I feel _____."
>
> *Art:* We taped the words "ANGRY" and "SAD" on the four sections of the easel and children painted pictures of how those emotions looked, times that they had felt that way, and what they did when they felt angry or sad.
>
> *Dramatic play:* Children built houses out of blocks and used our play people to act out fights and arguments and what happened after.

Table top: We put out small wooden cubes and teddy bear counters for the children to act out arguments and what might happen when arguments occur.

Before work time, I talked with Carlos to find out if there was an area where he would like to be in charge to recreate what [had] happened, with his friends around to help him work through it. He really liked that idea. "You mean I get to show what really happened?" he asked. He chose to be in charge in the dramatic play area. The other children rallied around the idea of Carlos being in charge. They wanted him to feel better about the whole thing.

Our work time was spectacular. Everyone had their own experiences to draw upon to enrich what was going on in each area. Magical conversations occurred between children at the easel as they were painting. At the table top, the "fight" pulled in more and more teddy bears until there were so many that the children decided to have the police come to stop it. Children were writing down their feelings at the writing table, as well as specific incidents where they had seen people fighting. In the dramatic play area, Carlos directed the construction of his house and how the fight occurred. The children with him had ideas about what the Carlos doll could do when he saw the fight; they were actually giving him strategies for how to cope with a situation like this in the future!

I am lucky to own a digital camera, so I took pictures of each of these areas during work time. At our afternoon circle, we talked about what happened in the areas and I took notes. I told the children that I was going to try to write on the computer what we had done so we could post it in our class. The next day a few children illustrated a few key pieces of our book and I assembled it that night: the writing, digital pictures, and student illustrations. We laminated it and posted it on the back of our easel so we could all see each page.

Several times throughout the year Carlos would talk about "that time that I was in charge in the blocks when my parents were fighting." He later told me that the students in our community are his friends and he knew they could make him feel better; that is why he shared that day. What a testament to the amazing children in our class and the safety they create for each other.

Kirsten understood right away that Carlos had said something very significant to the class. He had described a potent family scene and his feelings of fear. I have heard many teachers quickly dismiss similarly potent statements made by children in school, but Kirsten wants a classroom climate where children feel safe in expressing what is of true meaning to them.

Kirsten gave Carlos her full attention. She acknowledged his feelings of fear. She understood that the children listening might have stories similar to Carlos's or that they might feel worried that this could happen to them. She wanted to help all of the children explore and work through the powerful feelings that arise around a topic such as this, and to come to some sense of closure, even to feel that they might have good ideas about what to do in emotionally charged situations.

Kirsten and her student teacher spent time talking together about their own childhood experiences with family fighting, making space in their planning time for their own feelings. They designed curriculum activities that helped children construct their own understanding of conflict. They used simple, flexible materials, which allowed for children's experience to come forth in a dynamic mix with the ideas of others. The open-ended nature of the tasks they proposed invited children to bring their full personal and cultural identities into the process. There was room for the children to invent their own stories and to invent safe endings for them, to engage in the active process of meaning making through the kind of play that can transform and heal. This opened up an avenue to feelings of empowerment and generosity as children gave their own ideas and strategies to Carlos.

In these activities, academic skills such as literacy and math were connected to the meaningful content of children's lives, instead of being taught as isolated skills to be learned apart from experience. The book Kirsten made captured children's firsthand experience in writing and pictures. Deep personal meaning fueled the children's interest in literacy: the pages spoke of their reality in their own words.

Learning about Emotions in School

If we ground our curriculum in children's own meanings and in their experiences, then feelings will come to school along with thoughts. Because of exposure to cultural influences that are basically antisocial, many children will need help from teachers in connecting to their own feelings and to the feelings of others. For many children, school may be the only place where this learning can happen.

Even for teachers who want to connect to the inner lives of children, knowing how to do this is a real challenge. Most teacher education programs do not offer training in emotional literacy. And most of the literature on the topic offers little guidance for how to approach this work developmentally. How might teachers begin to encourage young children to express and learn about feelings in school?

Kirsten shows us how we might begin in the example above. She invites emotional experience into the classroom by how she listens to Carlos and the other children. This practice is sometimes called *active listening*—an approach that involves listening with acceptance and full attention, and reflecting back what is heard without judging it. Kirsten listens with openness and is fully present even when hard feelings get expressed. Because of how she listens, children are encouraged to look more deeply within. Perhaps we could say that Kirsten is listening with "soul," as Rachael Kessler puts it. When a teacher listens as Kirsten does, children learn that the sense that *they* make of things is important and that it is safe to express whatever they feel.

Teachers are notorious for not listening deeply to what children say, for hearing only what they want to hear, for evaluating what children say, for framing questions to get only the responses they want. It can be scary for a teacher to let go of his or her control over what will be said in class. This is especially hard when teachers are under extreme pressure to meet standardized requirements and so must impose more and more outside agendas on children.

Kirsten enlists the natural meaning-making capacities of children as she helps them develop emotional literacy. She begins with children's own emotional lives as her starting point and builds from there. Her work is developmentally rooted in how children see the world. When it comes to learning about emotions, developmental insights are a valuable guide.

Young children's thinking tends to be concrete, but feelings are abstract and can't be seen.[13] Children tend toward static thinking—having one idea at a time—so it is difficult for them to relate ideas logically in the emotional arena just as it is in other areas. Also extremely difficult for children is understanding how someone else feels. Even adults have a difficult time taking another perspective, but because of egocentric thinking, young children's minds are often filled with their own point of view.

These developmental ideas can be a starting point for identifying goals for working on emotional literacy with young children.

EMOTIONAL LITERACY GOALS FOR YOUNG CHILDREN

- Help children identify their feelings.
- Help children learn to "read" the feelings of others.
- Help children learn to express their feelings; help them develop a repertoire of words for feelings.
- Help children develop empathy for how others feel.
- Help children connect feelings to the actions and words that caused them.
- Help children separate feelings from action, to learn to think before acting.

Using these goals as a guide, teachers can invent a host of classroom activities that foster emotional literacy. Some teachers use "feeling photos"—pictures of faces expressing a range of emotions—as a way to make feelings more concrete. When children have actual conflicts, teachers point out how someone's face looks as a way to help a young child realize how the person feels.

Alison also teaches in an urban public school kindergarten. She made a book with her class of five-year-olds on the theme "how we feel and what makes us feel that way." Children wrote and drew pictures; Alison took photos of their faces showing how they felt and bound it all together into a beautiful book. One child wrote, "I feel furious because my brother keeps coming into my room and kicking my stuff around." And another wrote, "I feel frustrated when my mom knocks down my blocks and says, '*Oops, sorry*,' then I get frustrated."

Bill, who teaches second grade, used puppets to work on "put-down" statements with his students. Hurtful put-downs had been on the rise in his classroom, so Bill acted out a scene in which the puppets made comments to each other much like those Bill had heard the students using. He wanted to explore with children the feelings of hurt and what causes them. Here's part of the classroom discussion that followed:

LISA: My older brothers call me mean things, like they'll call me a monkey.
MONICA: My brother tells me my haircut doesn't look good.
LISA: It just makes me very sad.
JOEY: I feel baddest when someone says, "You're dumb" because it's *you* and when they say it about a thing it's just a *thing*.

LAURA: I have two older brothers and when they say that I feel really bad.

SHEA: Everyone is going to feel bad if you say that to them. It really hurts the person's feelings.

OMAR: *You* includes everything about you and it's not like anything you like, it's *you*. You're a bad person.

In the early childhood classrooms where I spend time to keep in touch with children and teachers, I always try to use developmental goals for emotional literacy as a guide for dealing with a conflict. One day Maya had just come into kindergarten not looking very happy. She headed for the attendance sheet to sign in, pencil in hand. But then she turned and poked Timothy with the eraser end of the pencil (he was not really hurt by this). I quickly took the pencil from Maya, but I didn't want to scold her; I wanted to show her how her actions had affected Timothy. I said, "Look Maya!" and poked the pencil into my own stomach, dramatizing how it hurt. Then I said to Maya, "It hurts when you poke someone with a pencil in the stomach." She looked at me very seriously, then resumed writing.

Later that morning Maya drew a picture all on her own. She dictated to the classroom aide, "I poked Timothy in the stomach with the pencil. Then I felt bad." Her teacher told me what a breakthrough this was for Maya. He had been very concerned about her frequent aggression toward other children and her seeming lack of awareness or empathy over having hurt them.

My assumption in this situation was that Maya, who was five years old, did not really understand how her jab felt to Timothy and that making a connection to how he felt could call forth that understanding. While many adults see their role with children as one of teaching right and wrong by *telling*, I wanted to teach by *showing*, to help Maya build her own connections to feelings. Many adults would say to Maya, "No, that's wrong to poke someone. You can't do that." Or they might send her to the time-out chair for a while to "think about" what she had done. But it's hard to think about what you've done if you don't really understand it. Children need our help in learning about how others feel in ways that fit with their developmental understanding. Working with them in this way gives us the best chance to open up their capacity to feel for others.

Nurturing a Spirit of Generosity

Recently I visited a preschool classroom where one of my students was practice teaching. At the end of the morning, as children were sitting with their coats on to go home, the head teacher took out some stickers and began handing them out to individual children and complimenting them on their good behavior that day. Three of the children didn't get stickers. One of them got very upset, cried, and pleaded for one. The teacher told him he hadn't behaved well enough that day, maybe he would get a sticker tomorrow. The child went out the door with a look of dejection.

It is painful to watch children's hurt and disempowerment in school situations like this. At the moment the stickers were dispensed, this little boy was filled with wanting one; how the sticker related to his behavior earlier in the day as seen by his teacher was not something he could comprehend, given his developmental understanding. Reward systems such as this one pervade schools, along with similarly divisive systems such as grading and ability groups. They undermine children's sense of safety and ability to form caring relationships with one another.

All children look for ways to feel competent and powerful in their lives. All too often, under the influence of a competitive school atmosphere backed up by antisocial media messages, they seek empowerment through teasing, bullying, or putting down other children. These behaviors offer a kind of fleeting, pseudo-power, a slim reward compared to the deeper, more sustaining sense of mastery that comes when we learn how to create positive relationships that engender feelings of joy and caring. In today's world, teachers need to take care to open up the channels for this to happen, and even to show children where and how to find these feelings with one another.

Over the course of the year that I visited Stuart's kindergarten class regularly, I saw him figure out how to build a classroom where genuine caring among children could thrive. First he introduced a set of structures for managing the classroom that children could learn to use on their own: a job chart, a list of daily tasks, activity centers—all rotating according to predictable schedules that the children could rely upon. This is a necessary first step—establishing a climate of predictability and fairness—toward building a social climate where feelings of genuine caring among children can develop.

When Alison joined Stuart at midyear as his intern, she brought new ideas for developing the social curriculum. She introduced conflict resolution skills, and the idea of a "conflict corner"—a place equipped with cozy cushions, paper for drawing, and puppets to use for safely acting out feelings, where children could go to talk over their conflicts. There were photos on the wall showing different ways children had resolved conflicts between themselves and their own words below each photo: "Share," "Cooperate," "Rub the hurt spot," "Take turns," "Say sorry." These gave children a repertoire of ideas for specific actions they could take to make things better. The children in this classroom began to feel a sense of empowerment about being able to solve their own problems; the more they did, the more they could do. On one of my visits, I heard Marcel, a child who'd had many behavior problems all year, say to two children who were arguing, "Do you two need to go to the conflict corner?"

Early in the spring, Alison suggested to Stuart that they introduce the idea of a "peace watch" to the children. They began simply, by noticing the helping behavior that occurred in the classroom and writing it down. Their list looked like this:

> Derrick rubbed Marcel's knee to make him feel good.
> Jamal let Kevin wear his hat so his head wouldn't be cold.
> Clarence helped Teresa tie her shoe.
> Janeen made Danisha feel good by rubbing her back.
> Adriana helped Jorge put away the snap cubes. It made Jorge
>   happy.
> When Wendy was crying, Leland gave her a hug and Christian
>   rubbed her knee.

Each day at class meeting children dictated new ways they had discovered to help each other. Then they began going up to the list during the day to add helpful acts to it in their own invented spellings or with Alison's help. Eventually the list grew down to the floor, so the class decided to start putting beans in a jar to mark the helpful acts instead— one bean for every act. When I got there, they were marveling at a jar already half full.

On my way into class that day, I walked through the coatroom and saw a five-year-old girl comforting a sad friend. Soon after, I noticed a boy who was playing with blocks offer one from his pile to another child; then I saw a child's arm go around another's shoulder. None of these acts was happening in the presence of the teachers. I hadn't observed anything like this on any of my previous visits.

The peace watch fostered caring connections among these children that must have felt very satisfying to them, because it seemed to have taken on a life of its own. As the helpful acts were described out loud and written down, Stuart and Alison's students gained a concrete understanding of what the abstract word "helping" actually means. Each could experience himself or herself as a "good person," someone who helps others. For some of the children, this was a new way to see themselves. The writing of the list in the children's own words and the repeated counting and estimation of the number of beans accumulating in the jar brought both literacy and math into the social curriculum.

Children need opportunities to help them discover the powerful energy unleashed by positive connection to others. This energy diminishes the appeal of the pseudo-satisfaction they might get when they use their power over others by teasing or hurting them. Teachers can intentionally set up classrooms to foster the kinds of experiences Alison and Stuart evoked in their classroom. In so doing, they will make available an expanse of joy and loving connection that can be an unlimited source of meaning and purpose for children.

The Inner Life of Teachers

The teachers described in this chapter have a lot in common. They are all teaching in urban public schools where academic achievement is a high priority, yet they are finding ways to build curriculum and skills starting from how the children themselves see things. These teachers all value social and emotional skills along with other basic skills that schools need to teach. And they all teach in a way that shares power *with* children rather than uses power *over* children.

There are many external obstacles—expectations put forth by administrators, parents, school boards, and state legislatures—that make it hard to teach this way. But there are internal obstacles as well.

It can be very scary to teach as these teachers do. They cannot predict everything that will happen in their day when so much emerges from the children. They have to trust that learning will happen when children have a say in what and how they learn. They have to trust that children can learn to regulate their own behavior, make choices, and join with teachers to solve all kinds of problems.

A student of mine described an incident she had observed during her student teaching internship:

> In our kindergarten class (it's a morning program) children come in and hang their coats up first in the coatroom, which has cubbies for their things. Then they enter the classroom. Last week, a little boy came into the classroom with his coat still on. The head teacher told him to go back outside and hang the coat up. The child didn't say anything. He just stood there. She told him again to take his coat off, that he couldn't come into the room until he did. He was still quiet. Finally the teacher said to him, "Go out to the coatroom. If you want to wear your coat, then you can't come into the classroom. You'll have to stay in the coatroom." The little boy went out to the coatroom and sat there. He stayed there for the entire day.

What happened inside this teacher to make her act this way? Was she angry? Fearful? Why did she see this child as an adversary? Her own internal obstacle, whatever it was, kept her from even asking him why he wanted to keep his coat on. If she had been able to reach toward the meaning that this action had for him, she could have begun the process of solving this problem *with* him. The child's need for autonomy and sense of empowerment could have been met through a positive process. Instead, he preserved his sense of self in the only way he could figure out to do—by sitting all day in the coatroom. For developmental reasons, young children have difficulty thinking of options other than the one directly in front of them. It is the teacher who must think creatively enough to prevent or break through power deadlocks such as this one.

Teacher education programs, with all of our theories and techniques, tend to focus on a great deal of content that is outside of our individual selves. In his timely book *The Courage to Teach* (1998), Parker Palmer asks us to find more balance between our inner selves as teachers and our emphasis on objective knowledge, intellect, and technique.

Especially in the area of teacher preparation commonly called "classroom management," teachers tool up with techniques and approaches to discipline that focus on how to control *children's* behavior. Framing the topic this way leaves little or no room for paying attention to the inner feelings and tensions that arise in teachers when we interact with children. When we focus our attention so narrowly, especially in ways that view children as unruly and needing to be controlled, we distance ourselves from them as well as from our own selves; then it becomes harder to connect to the deeper meanings and purposes that underlie children's behavior.

Alfie Kohn points out that most discipline programs show teachers how to get children to comply with instructions without encouraging reflection on whether a demand a teacher makes is *reasonable* from the point of view of the child. Had the teacher in the example above thought about this, she might have been able to see that at the very least this child needed to have some say in what happened to him. But perhaps there was an obstacle in the way of her seeing the child's point of view in this situation. Perhaps this teacher needed to ask herself some other questions first: How do I feel when a student challenges my authority? What happens inside of me when I feel myself losing control? How do I want to use my power with children?

Everything that a teacher does emanates from how this last question gets answered. Not only discipline decisions, but decisions about class routines, schedules, what gets studied and how, and the organization of space all are deeply rooted in who has the power and how it gets used. Looking at how and why we as teachers use our power with children would be a good place to begin exploring what Palmer calls the "inner landscape of a teacher's life." It might help us get beyond some of the internal obstacles that keep us from seeing more creative ways to teach. It might help us break down some of the barriers between ourselves and children and lead us into a bigger humanity that encompasses both children and ourselves.

These are difficult times for teachers. Outside forces such as state standards, high-stakes testing, and the influence of a violence-saturated commercial culture put conflicting pressures on teachers: just at the time when a more holistic, student-centered approach to learning is

needed it is becoming harder for teachers to provide it. The school
shootings and youth violence that fill the headlines highlight the need
for schools to implement effective social curriculum and programs
that reach every young person. For many children today, school may
be the only place where they can learn positive social and emotional
skills and experience a sense of connection to a larger community.

Even under the weight of conflicting political and cultural forces,
many teachers are finding ways to teach that draw in and nurture
every dimension of humanity that children bring to school. More
than ever before, we need teachers who can support children's active
learning, and classrooms where all dimensions of every child—including the emotional, social, and spiritual—can be seen, valued, and
nurtured. Moving in that direction means moving into the heart of
teachers too. As we look within and examine ourselves, we will be better able to take care of the whole of every child we work with, to use
our own empathy and compassion for children to dissolve the barriers
between heart and intellect, and to help them develop their spirits as
well as their minds.

LARRY BRENDTRO AND MARTIN BROKENLEG

The Circle of Courage:
Children as Sacred Beings

What would the world be to us
If the children were no more?
We should dread the desert behind us
Worse than the dark before.

—Henry Wadsworth Longfellow

A Cree elder from Canada shared with us one of the last conversations he had with his aging grandfather. "Grandfather," he asked, "what is the meaning of life?" After a period in thought, the old man answered, "Grandson, children are the purpose of life. We were once young and someone cared for us, and now it is our time to care."

Our worldviews are shaped by our cultural and family attachments. Each of us drags around a cultural tail a thousand years long, as well as our more personal family tales. Our own Lakota (Sioux) grandfather was born in the mid-1800s and did not see his first White man until after the encroachments of Custer's cavalry. He proudly carried the name Brokenleg, which memorialized an injury incurred in his job of training wild horses. Up until his death at ninety-nine years of age, he only spoke Lakota as he told us, his grandchildren, stories of our culture before we were subjugated by European settlers.

When the son of Grandfather Brokenleg reached "school age," he was captured and hauled away in one of the trucks that came each fall to our reservation from government or church-sponsored boarding schools. In Lakota culture each youth was given a unique name. However, the boarding school Brokenleg's son was taken to imposed European patriarchal customs, and someone there assigned this young boy

[39]

the surname of his father and the first name Noah. The motto of colonial education at the time was "Kill the Indian to save the child." These children, who had never experienced force dealt out in anger by an adult, were beaten if they spoke their native language.

The Europeans believed that Indian children were little primitives in need of socialization. In reality, they had brought with them a backward theory of child development, one that assumed that children were evil and had to be punished into submission. In contrast, our grandfather's people had sophisticated systems of child rearing that reflected the democratic principles they embraced. The goal of discipline was to teach courage instead of obedience. Elders used respectful communications with children to instill the values of being a good relative. In the words of a Lakota leader,

> The days of my infanthood and childhood were spent in surroundings of love and care. In manner, gentleness was my mother's outstanding characteristic. Never did she, nor any of my caretakers, ever speak crossly to me or scold me for failures or shortcomings. (Standing Bear, in *Land of the Spotted Eagle*)

Anthropologists have long been aware that North American tribal cultures had very different systems of discipline than the coercive obedience and harsh corporal punishment common in Western culture. At the core of the punitive mindset of the latter is a view of the child as inferior to the adult. If one were to say, "You are acting like a child," in any European language, this would be interpreted as an insult. In the Lakota tongue, this phrase would be, "You are acting like a sacred being," which is certainly not a put-down. When an early treaty was broken by the U.S. government, a Lakota chief remarked, "What would we expect from people who beat their sacred beings!"

We Are All Relatives

In traditional tribal kinship systems, the siblings of one's parents would also be mothers and fathers, and the persons Europeans call cousins would be brothers and sisters. Most everyone with white hair would be a grandparent. Similar kinship models exist among tribal peoples worldwide, as reflected in the African adage "It takes a village to raise a child" and the Cree belief "Every child needs many mothers."

Noted psychoanalyst Erik Erikson studied child rearing on our reservations to prepare a chapter in his book *Childhood and Society*, published in 1950. He was shocked to discover that some Sioux children didn't know who their "real" parents were until it came time to fill out the papers required for school admission. Lakota grandmothers did not share Erikson's concern that shared parenting was destructive to a child. In fact, they were more concerned about the poor little White kid who had only one mother—what would happen if that mother were too young, immature, or overwhelmed by her own problems?

Ella Deloria was a Lakota teacher and anthropologist who in her book *Speaking of Indians* described the spirit of belonging in Native American culture in this manner: "Be related, somehow, to everyone you know." The ultimate test of kinship was not genetic but behavioral: you belonged as a relative if you acted as if you belonged. Treating others as kin forged powerful human bonds that drew everyone into a network of relationships based on mutual respect.

The Circle of Courage

In 1988 we were asked by the Child Welfare League of America to make a presentation on Native American child development principles to an international conference in Washington, D.C. We called our synthesis of this research on tribal wisdom the Circle of Courage.

The Circle of Courage is represented as a medicine wheel, which is used by tribal peoples to illustrate that all must be in balance and harmony. The four directions of the Circle portray the four developmental needs of children: belonging, mastery, independence, and generosity. The various Native tribes do have many differences, but these four principles can be found in the traditional writings and practices of indigenous peoples throughout North America. These values grew out of cultures with structures markedly different from those of hierarchical European society.

In her book *The Chalice and the Blade* (1987), Riane Eisler contends that there are two basic models for human cultures, which she calls the dominator and the partnership paradigms. The dominator paradigm was the traditional model that appeared throughout much of European history. The partnership model may well have existed in European antiquity and is still seen in many tribal cultures that are organized around more democratic principles.

A comparison of the values found in these models is briefly summarized here:

1. *Belonging* is the organizing principle in partnership cultures. Significance is assured by belonging, whereas in dominator cultures one gains significance by standing out from the others, as seen in the hyperindividualism of U.S. society today.

2. *Mastery* measures competence by a person's progress relative to past performance rather than in comparison to others. The achievements of all are celebrated. In dominator cultures, "winners" show competence by beating "losers."

3. *Independence* is the only principle that allows all persons to exert power over their lives. In dominator systems, only a few can occupy coveted positions of power; the majority are obliged to submit.

4. *Generosity* is the measure of virtue in partnership cultures, where relationships are more important than possessions. In a dominator culture, the "good life" is reflected by the accumulation of material goods.

After we first presented this model in Washington, a participant in our session approached us privately to ask, with some shyness, whether perhaps the values embodied in the partnership paradigm were not exclusive to Indian cultures, but also formed the foundation underlying most ethical systems, such as those seen in first-century Christian communities. We would agree. In fact, developmental psychologists have found universal human patterns of what they speak of as attachment, achievement, autonomy, and altruism that correspond closely to the principles of the Circle of Courage.

In this materialistic, fast-paced culture, however, many children have broken circles, and the fault line usually starts with damaged relationships. Having no bonds to significant adults, young people chase counterfeit belongings through gangs, cults, and promiscuous relationships. Some are so alienated that they have abandoned the pursuit of human attachment. Guarded, lonely, and distrustful, they live in despair or strike out in rage. Families, schools, and youth organizations are being challenged to form new "tribes" for all of our children so there will be no "psychological orphans."

The Philosophy of a Circle of Courage School

Native North American children often drop out of school because the dominant culture contradicts important spiritual beliefs and traditions. Most tribal languages do not contain separate words for European concepts such as religion, education, or art, because in tribal culture all of these are seen as interrelated. Education and spirituality are not separate from, but intimately interwoven into, the fabric of daily living.

Our colleague Mohawk social worker Adrienne James notes that the medicine wheel symbolizes the circle of life, its unity, and the interrelatedness of all its dimensions. The four directions of the circle can be interpreted in various ways:

Four forms of life: human, animal, plant, and mineral
Four elements: earth, air, water, and fire
Four races: red, black, yellow, and white
Four winds, Four seasons, Four directions—and so on

Humans also have four dimensions: spiritual, emotional, physical, and mental. Healthy survival, or "good medicine," requires that balance and harmony be always maintained. If spirituality is left out of our lives or teaching, we ignore an essential part of our being and the circle is broken.

Therefore spirituality is infused into the learning environment of a Circle of Courage school. In such a school, spirituality involves developing and maintaining a sense of belonging to all that surrounds us. Students must develop the mastery and competency of which they are capable, and they must do this with a sense of sharing and cooperation rather than hoarding and selfish competition.

Achievement and success in the Western tradition is grounded in egoistic motivation. In contrast, the Native American view of success is that everyone has special gifts and competencies. When one person demonstrates a particularly high level of achievement, this is not regarded as representing a victory over others but as a role model or goal to emulate. The high achiever is to be congratulated and praised for achievement but not at the price of demeaning others by making them "losers."

The Western view is that humans are destined to conquer nature, while Native spirituality views all of creation as part of the whole and sees our survival as dependent upon harmony and balance throughout the universe. These values conflict with those of a materialistic society. Of course schools must prepare students for economic survival, but spirituality can provide an alternative to the dominant culture's stress on competition and accumulation beyond need. The challenge is to help our children learn that economic development and their life vocation must be shaped by cultural values, kinship and community bonds, shared responsibilities and benefits, and respect for the environment.

Some people might argue that including spirituality in a tax-supported school is an unconstitutional "establishment of religion." We believe that such is not the case, because there is a distinction between recognizing and supporting spirituality and propagating or establishing a particular religion. The foundation for our spirituality is the belief that all children are sacred spiritual beings, and our responsibility as older brothers and sisters is to enhance and nurture them.

Spirituality is present in school settings, whether we recognize it or not, because people by nature are spiritual. By incorporating this into our teachings, we enable our children and all our people to live our traditions and culture as we believe they should be lived. As we mend our broken circle, we maintain harmony and balance for all of Mother Earth's inhabitants.

Listening to Spiritual Voices

An old Native American man was down on the ground interacting with a tiny child. His relatives said to him, "Grandfather, what are you doing crawling around on the ground like a little child?" He responded, "I am very old and some time soon I will be going to the spirit world. This child is very young and has just come from the spirit world. I am down here seeing what I can learn from this sacred being."

There is a new confluence between the secular and the spiritual in contemporary society. In the recent past, spiritual issues were pushed out of public life at least partly because of the damage caused by religious conflicts in a diverse culture. Bill Moyers, a former Baptist clergyman and presidential press secretary, addressed this dilemma in his PBS television series on religion and diversity, asking, Can a pluralistic United States avoid the bitter fruits of religion, such as intolerance and fanaticism, that have driven people apart? Can we instead form a sense of community of shared spirituality that contributes to justice and mutual respect?

Moyers sees the solution to religious tensions as depending on our ability to listen to people whose experience and reality may be different from ours. He maintains that we need not abandon our own distinctive traditions; rather, through critical encounters with others as persons of faith we can be enriched by what he calls the "religious mosaic" of our nation.

Throughout history and in most cultures, spiritual wisdom was passed on from the elders to the young. It was assumed that those most experienced in living would share essential concepts about the meaning of life through example and precept. Today, elders in traditional tribal cultures still pass on the stories and values that keep the culture alive. In modern civilizations, however, rapid social changes have left older generations feeling confused and ignorant about the world in which their children and grandchildren must live. At the same time, younger generations in our society have not been socialized to honor the experience of their elders. This effectively cuts youth off from the primary source of wisdom concerning the meaning of life, leaving each new generation to stumble alone in the dark without expert spiritual mentors.

Dr. Karl Menninger capped a distinguished psychiatric career by founding the Villages to serve children "who have no belongings." We once asked Dr. Menninger which of his many books was the most important. He suggested that *The Vital Balance* (1963), although not as well known as some of his other books, would have the most enduring significance. This work describes how healthy emotional adjustment requires living in harmony with one's inborn nature. When lives are out of balance, dysfunction occurs in forms of stress, personality problems, aggression, psychosis, and even self-destruction. Menninger believed that modern society is less successful in meeting the basic needs of children than simpler cultures have been: "Consider these children to have fallen among thieves," he wrote in 1982, "the thieves of ignorance and sin and ill fate and loss. Their birthrights were stolen. They have no belongings."

Children who lack the foundations for self-esteem live in perpetual stress, for their lives are out of balance. They flail out at a world that has not given them respect, or they internalize the message that they are worthless. A seventh grader named Jerome from the Pine Ridge Indian reservation describes children with broken circles of courage in simple and powerful language:

> I want to be treated with respect and dignity. If you respect me, I will respect you. If you take pride in me, I will take pride in you. But if you treat me bad I will probably abuse myself by drugs, alcohol, and low self-esteem. This is going to all the parents on earth. Give us love and attention, listen to us when we have a problem and talk to us when you have a problem. Because when you ignore us, it makes us feel stupid and mad. It feels bad when we get hurt by bad names, teasing, taunting, and being ignored. So, talk it over with somebody and tell your kids you love them.

Listening to the Voices of Youth

"The market value of the very young is small," wrote Janusz Korczak, of Poland. "Only in the sight of God and the Law is the apple blossom worth as much as the apple, green shoots as much as a field of ripe corn."

Korczak was the preeminent advocate for marginalized children in the early twentieth century. He set up self-governing schools for street children, and he castigated both the capitalist and communist systems for treating children as economic resources rather than as persons with dignity. In *The Child's Right to Respect* (1929), he challenged adults to listen to young people and involve them in the creation of their educational communities.

Students in courage-building schools are not coerced into obedience but participate in partnerships of mutual respect. A number of years ago, we began asking students about how the Circle of Courage values might apply to their schools. As they have told us, many students find these positive experiences, such as belonging, in their schools, but this is often incidental rather than a result of intentional interventions. A significant number do not, and these include alienated young people who desperately need a positive school climate.

The insightful comments of these students indicate that young people have important contributions to make in identifying and solving the problems of their schools. In fact, when youth are not in an alliance with adults, they often use their considerable talents in adversarial and defiant behavior; those who distrust adults employ sophisticated strategies to attack, avoid, or outwit authority figures. If young people are clever enough to sabotage our educational efforts, they are mature enough to be involved in building positive school communities.

Dr. Edna Olive has directed alternative schools for African-American youth in the Washington, D.C., area, schools in which the Circle of Courage philosophy has been the unifying theme of the programs offered. Recently she interviewed students from the Florence Burtell Academy of Prince George's County about how the values of the Circle have affected their lives. She chose the following quotes to share here:

Kevin, on mastery:

So I had to pass this test to get in [the Navy]. So to let you know how much I appreciate and love the staff at FBA [Florence Burtell Academy], they realized, a lot of academic staff and my teachers, they realized that this was something I want to do and I know that I had to also get my high school diploma. I had to do the work to get my high school diploma in order to go into the military. So not only do I have to pass the test, I have to get my diploma, so they incorporated the test work into school work and I did that for a good while. I managed to get into the service 'cause I passed the test. My math score increased from the last time I took the test, my reading and English score increased. The science part increased since the last time I took it 'cause I didn't know much about volume and liters, I wasn't into that stuff, but I got into studying at each individual class at FBA and the teachers, they helped me . . . they helped me a whole lot.

Eric, on belonging:

Well this is the only comfortable place I know. I can't stay in that laundry room all day, I can't stay in that building all day, and the school is a comfortable setting for me. I can laugh with people. I know, I can, you know, relax. I can't have two bad places, home and school, 'cause that was like hell all around. This was like a family-oriented atmosphere. Definitely people care at this school. The teachers care as well as educate, the counselors care as well as facilitate behaviors. School helped a lot, like the therapists and counselors. They care, genuinely. Some of the actions they display tell me. They tell me to get out of the halls not just because someone will come along and say the halls have to be clear. They tell me to go to class because they want me to do good, they want to see you excel well, they don't want to see you just go down the drain. They genuinely care. It's there, you can see it in their conversation. They let me come into the classroom and do extra work. It's hard to explain, it's just there. I did well at school because I have attachments to the people at school. These things helped me and kept me going. The school is strong and well disciplined, and I made it through.

Damien, on generosity and independence:

In the nursing home, I clean people. I would take this man out of his seat, put gloves on and clean him after the toilet. It makes me feel good to help people. I feel proud of myself, I feel love. I have big dreams of making money and opening up a nursing home myself. My calling is to help people. That's who I am right now, just to help people. And to give a service to someone, you give a service to someone, you give a service and do it to the best of your ability. And that's my calling and missionary work. There are a lot of people here who have taken me under their wings in a positive direction. Now, it's not even money! It's just helping someone. I want to be known, not for myself. My mission and my goals are never just for me. I got a point where I want to get money but never just about me. So when I see people, I want to help. I don't just do anything to be famous but to help. I want to help kids like this school helped me. I have learned an ultimate gift that I can do things for myself. I know that the same amount that you put in is the amount you will get back.

Each of these young men has experienced the tenets of the Circle of Courage. The staff at this therapeutic day program live and model the Circle of Courage each day. "Relationships, autonomy, helping one another, and giving are at the center of our work with the students," Dr. Olive says, "and we understand that the process must be reciprocal. Students are always learning. However, are we as adults always teaching what we want them to live and learn?"

Many students come to Florence Burtell after other programs have failed them, both emotionally and academically. While staff members understand the formal model of the Circle of Courage and discuss its principles often, the students understand it through their experiences at the school. The frequent use of the words *family, fairness, learning, understanding, progress, giving, helping, growing, role model, respect,* and *responsibility* by these students provides evidence of the re-claiming environment which is spoken of in the Circle of Courage model. Perhaps one of the most vivid examples of the success of this approach at Florence Burtell is the quarterly Recognition Day, which celebrates the efforts of students in all facets of the program, including social behavior, academics, community living and participation, athletics, and the performing arts. "On this day," writes Dr. Olive, "the transformation unfolds."

> The spirit of mastery is seen as students who have never passed a standardized test before receive recognition for passing all required functional academic tests for high school graduation. The spirit of belonging resounds as students give each other standing ovations, scream, shout, and cheer because a member of their school family has received recognition. In the spirit of generosity, students thank one another and the staff for giving them the support and courage needed to accomplish their goals. The spirit of independence is dem-onstrated in the positive choices they are making for their living and learning as autonomous and responsible young adults.

In recounting their own stories of transformation and reclaiming, Dr. Olive tells us, Eric, Kevin and Damien speak to a spirit and presence guiding their lives and their choices. This awareness has come to them in many different ways and in many different places. Kevin uses a Christian vocabulary to describe it:

> Like it reminds me of that story Daniel and the Lion's Den and overcoming a big battle you know? Jesus helped him, and he helped me overcome a major, major battle and was life-threatening. But he gave me a reason to live, he put it back in me. He put the will to live back in me and to change it around and do a new thing. God can do it, only you got to want to do it for yourself, too. He gave me another chance. I mean a God of more than second chances. He had a plan for me and I got here. I got to this school. I know that if God hadn't put FBA in my life when he did I would have failed. So I truly thank the Lord for calling these people, and I thank the entire staff—administrators, so-cial workers, teachers, counselors, assistants, and everyone—for answering God's call.

Enlisting youth in improving their lives and schools is only possible in a climate of mutual respect. This requires valuing the strengths and potentials of all students, even those with broken circles. Schools and youth organizations that fail to nurture the spirit of belonging, mastery, independence, and generosity are inadvertently fostering discouragement. Some might argue that it is not the business of schools to address the spiritual dimension. This would be a plausible argument only if one assumes that children are not sacred beings.

Creating Communities of Courage

> I do not ask whether my wounded brother suffers. I will myself be this wounded brother.
> —Walt Whitman

The most practiced phrase in the Lakota language is *Mitakuye oyasin,* which means "we are all relatives." Lakota people invoke this beatitude of belonging on almost any pretext to remind us to always respect one another. Upon greeting, we prime our conversation by pronouncing kinship bonds, by calling each other "Son" or "Grandmother." If we are clueless about how we are related, we call that person "Cousin." Being a genuine relative is based not on a blood test but on a test of generosity.

Treating others as brothers and sisters is a theme common to all great religious traditions. However, this idealistic value has often been subordinated to other values in Western civilization, those which celebrate dominance and selfish materialism. Biblical texts may prescribe a millstone around the neck for drowning those who violate children, but the history of childhood shows that children were routinely enslaved, indentured, or discarded. Old forms of abuse have been largely eliminated, but 80 per cent of American youth report that adults in their communities don't support them.

Many tell us that the beauty of the Circle of Courage is its simplicity. One does not have to develop elaborate schemes to nurture belonging, mastery, independence, and generosity, because this is really getting back to human basics. The Circle of Courage is not a program to be standardized, field-tested, and disseminated. It does not provide the answers, but rather helps us pose the right questions so that we can discover the answers within ourselves. For example, we inform our undergraduate student teachers that an upcoming test will require listing twenty ways to create a more belonging school, and none has ever failed to do so, even though they have not yet completed their training. Circles of Courage is an intentionally creative activity.

Every successful program for youth needs a core of beliefs and values that tie staff and young people together. Perhaps the most useful contribution the Circle of Courage has made is to provide such a unifying theme, one that can be used to support a wide variety of teaching and treatment philosophies. The Circle points us to the most important goals. Once we are certain what we believe, we are able to choose from a wide range of methods that might achieve these ends in various settings and circumstances.

The motto of the Green movement is "Think globally, act locally." So it is with creating Circles of Courage. Cathann Kress of Cornell University is working with the National 4-H organization to develop Circle of Courage violence prevention models in communities and schools. Don Jacobs of Oglala Lakota University on the Pine Ridge reservation is developing a character education program based on the Circle. Frank Fecser and the staff of the Positive Education Program for disturbed children in Cleveland are replacing traditional "level systems" with one based on Circle of Courage principles. Youth programs in Canada, South Africa, Australia, and New Zealand have used our models in working with indigenous youth, and Richard Villa and Jacqueline Townsend employ the Circle's principles as they work for the inclusion of special education students. On a broader level, the annual Black Hills Seminars on Reclaiming Youth bring together practitioners, policy leaders, and youth to explore leading-edge programs, and new Circle of Courage initiatives are featured in the journal *Reclaiming Children and Youth*.

Thinking globally and acting locally means creating "new tribes" in which all can live in respect and harmony—the meaning of the circle. To underscore what we mean by "courage," we will end this essay with the voice of fifth grader Echo Le Beau. Echo attends a parochial school on the Pine Ridge reservation in one of the poorest counties in the United States. She writes with a resilience of spirit and a solid sense of self-worth, challenging adults to approach all young persons as sacred beings:

> Treat me with respect, the way you would to a person who you look up to. Teach me things from right to wrong. Understand me and have patience with me when I'm having hard times. Be proud of me when I do things right. When something does go wrong, show me the right way without getting mad. When your anger flares up, put your hands in your pocket and don't use them on me. Remember, I am a gift to you from God, you are a gift to me from God, and His love is always there for us to share.

LAURA PARKER ROERDEN

Lessons of the Wild

There is a spiritual foundation that all of us were
born with. It is inherent to every kind of people,
a spiritual connection to this earth, to this land.

—Audrey Shenandoah,
a clan mother of the Onondaga Nation

We are scuba diving with twelve teenagers off Grand Cayman Island on what is called simply the Wall—a sheer vertical drop that begins in seventy feet of water and plummets into a dark abyss until it merges with the continental shelf at the depth of twelve thousand feet. We have stopped our descent at ninety feet, where the light penetrating from the surface supports an abundance of marine life. Bright red corkscrew sponges, thick like rope, spiral up toward the light. On the brink of a coral ledge, a delicate purple vase sponge sits tilted as if frozen in a pose of falling. Hundreds of chromis, tiny blue jewel-tone fish, move in unison. The school's angular movements reflect the light in a shimmering display like a stained glass window. Other than the exaggerated sound of my own rhythmic breathing through a regulator, it is absolutely silent.

It is our students' first dive on the Wall. Their response is not unlike that of other groups we've brought here. Several dive pairs are hovering motionless over the abyss, face down to the shadowy darkness, seemingly stunned. Two girls have linked arms and are slowly traveling along the line of the top of the Wall as if they were spacewalking. Another two have thrust their flashlights and heads into a crevice. Students are paired for safety. We are diving as a group. But surveying the scene, the prevalent sense is that each of us is absorbed in his or her own deeply personal experience.

I direct a summer marine biology program in the Caribbean called Ocean Matters. This five-week course brings together between twelve and twenty high school–age students from around the world to explore the ecology of a Caribbean coral reef. My co-teacher Chris Gawle and I provide both classroom and field instruction on general marine science and coral reef ecology; a dive staff of two certifies students in scuba. We dive on the coral reef daily. The students design and execute a group research project that contributes to the general monitoring of the health of the reef and is later presented to the local department of the environment. They learn the Latin and common names of more than one hundred reef flora and fauna and explore complex theories of ecology and biology. For twelve to fifteen hours a day, we eat, sleep, and breathe science and the sea.

People have told me I'm crazy to bring adolescents to depths of a hundred feet with nothing but a tank of air on their backs and a couple of weeks of diving lessons under their belts. And sometimes I think they might be right. Each year I approach the coming of the program with a degree of apprehension. The stakes are high. What if someone gets hurt? Will we be able to establish the sense of individual and group responsibility that is vital to everyone's safety? And I worry that my expectations for the program are too lofty. Will this year be as successful as others? Will the experience change my students' lives as it has mine? In a way, bringing young people to a special place like the coral reef can be like introducing your parents to your future spouse. Will they come to love the reef as much as I do?

But never fail, something surprising and wonderful happens. In the dark fall and winter months, I am buoyed by postcards, e-mails, and visits from students who participated in previous years, telling me how the experience has made a difference in their lives. One girl tells me she is going to college after graduation instead of getting married because she now has the confidence she can do it. A boy writes that he's weathering the storm of his father's death better because he now understands that "nature's rhythms must echo in [his] life." Still others talk passionately about their decisions to pursue a career in marine sciences, "devoting my life to the sea" as one girl describes it.

Some equate the experience to that of falling in love. "I'll never be the same," another girl tells me with a knowing glance. And I know what she means. I don't really understand why the experience is so profound for some young people. But I have learned to rely on this: nature's strange alchemy resounds within children's souls.

Nature as Healer

> Those who contemplate the beauty of the earth find
> reserves of strength that will endure as long as life
> lasts. —Rachel Carson

Jake had been kicked out of three schools before he landed in our Caribbean program one summer. "See if you can fix him," his mother told me. I laughed at first. She was joking, right? But then I saw she wasn't, and I understood that Jake was up against more than just several schools that saw him as a failure. Our program is rigorous academically, and Jake came in barely meeting the minimum requirements. He was withdrawn and angry. He hadn't chosen to come to the program, he told me, his mother had wanted a "summer off" from him.

Jake found himself in a group of eleven other students who, he noted, were very different than his friends at home. He had recently been in rehabilitation for drug and alcohol addiction; he was considering dropping out of school altogether. Only months before he had extricated himself from a gang and still bore a tattoo of its insignia on his ankle like a dark shadow.

Our first two weeks with Jake were rocky. From the start he seemed to be challenging us, saying with his actions, "Come on, prove me a failure again." He had violated several program rules and was in danger of being expelled. Then something happened. Jake's turn-around was somewhat sudden, and it caught everyone off-guard—including maybe even Jake.

One day on a routine dive to collect data, Jake found a reef shark sleeping in the crevice of a coral balmy. He shared the discovery with all the students who were diving nearby, which, I should explain for anyone who hasn't been scuba diving, is no small feat. He swam tò each of his peers, rapped on their tanks or waved in their faces to get their attention, and then personally escorted them over to the shark. It took several trips back and forth before he had shared his discovery with everyone. That day Jake did not leave the water alone, as he usually did. Instead he emerged with several other students, triumphantly hooting and high-fiving. His expression was one of joy—and also of vulnerability. "It was the coolest thing I've ever seen," he said. And the others agreed. Jake was now part of the group. From here on in, his confidence soared. By the end of the program, he had earned the admiration of his peers and teachers, an honors-level grade in a college-level course, and the nickname MacGyver, after the capable TV detective who could find his way out of any problem. As we prepared to head home, Jake talked a lot about the high school he hoped to attend in Vermont, which had an outdoor education focus.

As educators, we can't resist analyzing such success stories as Jake's. What went right? we would ask in faculty meetings. We'd be convinced it was something we were doing programmatically: it's because we put him in charge of making the quadrats—the large contraptions made from PVC piping and wires for data collection—that he was gaining confidence, we'd tell each other. But Jake was like the artful dodger. Each time we thought we had him figured out, he'd prove us wrong. We were forced to acknowledge that perhaps what was working with Jake might have little to do with us. In fact, what was working seemed almost to require that we step out of the way. Would it be too radical to consider that nature itself was healing Jake?

Numerous studies of outdoor adventure programs similar to Ocean Matters suggest that successes like Jake's are not isolated incidents; this research shows widespread gains for youth in important internal constructs such as self-concept, self-efficacy, and self-actualization.[1] The theory is that these gains are predicated on an element of risk inherent to being in nature that the young person successfully navigates. Overcoming one's fears by successfully facing the challenges of the natural world can be very empowering. Kasha was a shy and somewhat physically awkward young woman when she entered the Ocean Matters program. Over time, we watched as she faltered and then gradually gained a confidence and grace in the water that seemed to carry over into her social and academic life. At the close of the experience, Kasha had this to say: "The program gave me more self-confidence and a higher self-image—the ability to say, 'Yes, I can do this'—by giving me a challenge I didn't think I could handle and letting me prove to myself that I *could* handle it, and do it well." Like Jake, she had faced and successfully met significant and deeply personal challenges—earning the acceptance of peers, the rigors of the academic work, the physical demands and dangers inherent in diving, and even, perhaps, the challenge of self-acceptance. Freed of the confines of classrooms, many young people experience for the first time a sense of themselves as powerful, or discover talents long dormant or previously undeveloped.

Of course it's true of every challenge we pose to children: they are opportunities for growth. But it was in working with Jake that I first began to appreciate just how fundamentally different outdoor challenges can be. As a scuba diver, Jake excelled. He moved gracefully in the water and had a natural ability to maintain his buoyancy. And there was a different quality about Jake *after* dives. His normally wiry and tense body was more relaxed; he was quiet but not brooding. He seemed more introspective and at peace. Even more intriguing, he possessed an uncanny ability to find interesting sea life in cryptic places.

When I asked Jake about what made him stop while we were diving together to examine a particular coral head where he had spotted a huge spiny lobster hiding in a hole, he said, "I don't know. I just had a feeling and I trusted it." I remember at the time being struck by the simple wisdom in that comment. On rare occasions this has happened to me in the water, too, as when I've felt a presence behind me and turned around to see a green turtle—my favorite coral reef resident—pass in the distance. Those moments might be dismissed by some as just dumb luck. But when it happens, it always feels to me a bit more like the way Jake described it—as some state of grace I have entered where I perceive things more keenly, where I am now looking at the world from the inside of the experience rather than from the outside.

Students often describe such connections to wildlife as eliciting deep emotions. After seeing an eagle ray, a beautiful member of the stingray family that soars through the water the way its namesake the eagle rides the tide of the wind, Kasha fished for words to explain her feelings about the experience. "The creature was just so elegant," she said. "It's hard to describe the emotions that come with the picture. But it's the emotions that make it powerful and different from anything I have ever experienced."

This return to being in our bodies, uniting mind, spirit, emotions, and our physical selves, is described by David Orr in his landmark book *Ecological Literacy* as an "embodied knowing."[2] It is a deeper knowledge than intellectual understanding. It is more akin to instinct or intuition. In nature, we are impelled from within to respond—we are drawn out of the shell of civilization that most of us wear, into a more authentic state. The turtle moves and my senses are stirred. I am like the wild animals we observe daily in their natural habitat: I too am vigilant, awake, alert. When such challenges call us to reach into the deepest parts of our souls, we often find we are connected to something larger than we are—something wild at its source.

Echoes of the Soul

> To an extent still undervalued in philosophy and religion, our existence depends on [our] propensity [towards other life], our spirit is woven from it, hope rises on its currents. —E. O. Wilson

We are teaching science, we try to remind ourselves. But even with this determined focus, lines blur. Larger questions and insights about the meaning and purpose of life always seem to emerge. Who am I? What is my place in this world? are at the heart of students' journal entries and late-night conversations on the beach. Where do I end and the world begin? Isn't it arbitrary that we draw the line of ourselves at the edge of our faces? Couldn't the giant "I" that we each are also encompass that tree, the ocean, the stars?

Students often describe their experience on the reef as one might talk about a very special personal relationship. Nature has a living presence in their lives. When I first met Eli he seemed offbeat and irreverent and I foolishly assumed that these qualities could not coexist with any amount of insight and sensitivity. I was wrong, of course. I learned from Eli that if we listen very closely we can hear nature speaking in our lives. "I think nature has a much stronger voice in my life today," he explained to me in a letter. "Depending on the day of the week or the situation, it is the voice of restraint, the voice of practicality, the voice of kindness. Sometimes it keeps me from doing something I might want to do . . . other times it makes me feel good about what I am doing."

Dave's father had died a few months before he came to the program, and it's likely that at the time he was suffering from an undiagnosed clinical depression. He described his experience with Ocean Matters as transformational and profound: "The program seemed to take me up into the womb again, which was the setting of our small society. After the program I was birthed into our world with a new life force inside of me: it was a passion for the beauty of everything in our world, with a consciousness of its fragility."

Dave's use of a birthing metaphor here is interesting on many levels. Perhaps it is not a coincidence that after being daily suspended weightless in sea water (approximating the same saline composition as amniotic fluid) Dave should think of birth. Or that his own rebirth should come at a time when he was grappling with death. Even our language acknowledges earth as the source of life: the word "nature" comes from a form of the Latin *nasci*, meaning "to be born."

Was nature in some way a mirror for Dave—a place where he could look deeply into the world, see his own soul reflected, and from this create meaning for his life? Dave seemed to think so. He would often sit alone on the shore after dinner. While at times we worried that he wasn't doing his homework, we let him be. It was clearly more important to him than we had known. Later he wrote:

> One evening, as the last remnants of the Caribbean sunset faded against the horizon, I found myself in a lounger out by the iron shore, looking inland. I sat there in a meditative trance staring at our hotel. As my thoughts deepened and the sky darkened, one distraction—the fluorescently lit Pepsi machine— irritated my sight. Unknowingly, I had picked up a broad leaf with imperfections. I held the leaf up to obstruct the Pepsi machine. The leaf glowed and I saw briefly my course in our world.

What we see when we look into nature is, admittedly, not always pretty. As Gary Snyder writes, "To acknowledge that each of us at the table will eventually be part of the meal is not just being 'realistic.' It is allowing the sacred to enter and accepting the sacramental aspects of our shaky temporary personal being." Nature is decay, putrefaction, imperfection, impermanence. It is unpredictable. It leads us to the edge of things and asks us to peer into what we thought was the void and later come to know as something else. It asks us to see ourselves differently. Too often, kids like Jake see themselves in the disapproving faces of their peers and teachers who at every turn seem to be telling them they are somehow bad, somehow flawed. Had Jake, like Dave, seen his reflection in nature, where imperfections are part of its dazzling beauty?

The Call of the Wild

Not long ago, I was at the rocky north shore of Massachusetts when I saw two young children crouching over a tide pool. They were both leaning over the dark unknown of the water with intent and concentration. "It's *alive!*" one boy exclaimed triumphantly as he thrust a wiggling green crab into the face of his companion. In his excitement the first boy dropped his pail, which a supervising parent patiently reclaimed from the surf. Both children then hung their heads in an attitude of prayer as they leaned closer and peered intensely at the creature. "Get the pail," one ordered. "We need to put it in water. It's *alive*, Mommy!" They both squealed in delight. And I too was caught up in the excitement. They hadn't been in a nature program. They weren't being led by a "knowing" adult. They were simply doing what comes naturally when children play outside.

Yet fewer than 10 percent of our children in the United States today learn about nature by being *in* nature. More than half learn about the natural world through technology and the rest from inside a classroom. The malaise we see in our children might, in fact, have much to do with this dislocation. As David Orr offers, "The sum total of violence wrought by people who do not know who they are because they do not know *where they are* is the global environmental crisis."[3] This is a crisis of spirit.

What is so healing about spending time in nature is the sense of "recovery" it brings—the sense of restoring ourselves to some primal state or, as the Buddhists refer to it, of being "in right relationship to all living things." You can almost hear a collective sigh of relief from our program's students as much of what we think of as civilization starts to fall away over the five weeks we are on the island.

At first they complain about not having a television set, or say they are bored. The Game Boys and Walkmans come out of their suitcases. This usually lasts less than a week, however, before a spirit of creativity, passion, and playfulness takes over. Students invent games; create crazy clothes and hats from things found in nature; watch sunsets; draw in their journals. They dance. Laugh. Go barefoot in the sand. They create myths not unlike those found in indigenous cultures, although with decidedly modern twists. The rock crabs bite them, they conjecture, because they are trying to sample their DNA and create a crab people; just last night, they say, Eli was carried off and replaced by a crab. And perhaps Eli in some way *was* replaced by a crab—the spirit of crab has entered his soul, transforming him and the others, bringing them into a more integrated state with nature.

Hannah, a quiet, seemingly average student who possessed extraordinary insight, summed up what she learned in the program with one word: humility. I couldn't have said it better myself. Young people's questions, insights, and honesty about nature always seem to snap me in half, making me acknowledge how small and insignificant I am. In a world where so little can be known, this thought is oddly comforting.

A Third Presence

Since we were working within the midst of one of the most complex and highly diverse ecosystems on earth—the coral reef—we chose to orient our study to the reef's ecology. That is, we studied the reef as a community, investigating the complex relationships among its members, as well as the relationship between the reef's inhabitants and their environment. Studying an ecosystem in its entirety has its advantages. Drawing the parameters for our inquiry—what we would study, what we wouldn't—was easy. The limits were drawn for us by the limits of the reef itself. We would study it all, we decided, as the reef revealed itself to us. What we didn't know when we first started this line of inquiry was how important ecology would become as a metaphor for what we as a human community were learning about ourselves.

For most students, it's difficult to consider the whole without first considering its parts. In their first moments on the reef, young people are preoccupied with its glitziest residents, the tropical fish.

Gradually, though, as they come to know the names of individual fish species, they begin to form questions about the relationships among the fish and the other life on the reef, and about the larger system. Why is it common to see damselfish hiding within an anemone? they might ask. (The damselfish has evolved an immunity to the poisonous tentacles of the anemone, which provide it with safe refuge from predators.) This leads us to investigations of other symbiotic relationships on the reef. As these are revealed among an increasing number of reef inhabitants, what is made visible is the very fabric of life. The reef has shape, texture, detail. Students' questions now become deeper and progressively more focused. How is it that such an abundance of life can live in such nutrient-poor waters as those of the tropics? What created and now sustains the high levels of diversity on the reef? John Muir once described what they discover: "When we try to pick out anything by itself we find it hitches to everything in the universe."

Over time, many students come to realize that the degradation of the coral reef has as much to do with the number of SUVs we drive in the United States as it does with shoreline development among the mangroves on the leeward side of the island. They come to see the reef as if it were an orchestra in which each member has an important and complementary role. The reef could no more sustain life if you removed all of the herbivores than an orchestra could play a symphony if you removed all the string players. As Eli pointed out, "The world is incredibly interconnected." There is only one ocean, not seven. There is only one earth.

This shift to a focus on the community over the individual in our studies of the reef creates a heightened appreciation for the interdependence among the members of our group. While it's tempting for us as faculty to make the analogy ourselves to students—to point out that our group is like an ecosystem; each member is valued, has a part to play; everyone's actions affect the others and the whole; diversity stabilizes the system—we've learned to be patient. As with all good, deep, and real learning, students must discover this truth for themselves. The reef reveals itself, underscoring our interdependence more deftly than any activity we teachers could devise. Eli spoke at length about this interdependence and the powerful memory he had of his dive on the Wall. "The Wall dive is by far the most vivid experience of my life," he explained. "Seeing the things we have been studying in a very special way, having my life dependent on people I love in a very real way, and looking off the Wall. Wow. That is a memory."

Ecology and the earth's ways help us to understand ourselves in terms of others, require us to learn how to resolve differences, ask us to listen, communicate, and value diversity. "The program . . . taught me a lot about dealing with others," Hannah said, "leadership, being cooperative, adjusting to circumstances, listening to what others have to say, and learning from them." In the words of the poet Mary Oliver, time in nature "announces our place in the family of things." For adolescents, this sense of belonging provides a much-needed refuge from the looming responsibilities of autonomy.

When you teach outside, what I think of as a "third presence" emerges, guiding and informing the learning—the earth itself will seemingly have a voice. When I've surrendered to this feeling, I've noticed my own passions reawakened. I've found the job of being all-knowing teacher impossible—nature reveals herself as too complex. Mysteries I do not yet understand reengage me as a learner. My sense of wonder and curiosity is renewed. Nature is not only the classroom, it is the teacher. The earth protects us, nurtures us, tells us about the shape of our heart, and we in kind are called to do the same for the earth.

Taking Action

> We are all one in nature. Believing so, there was in
> our hearts a great peace and a willing kindness for all
> living, growing things. —Luther Standing Bear

Whole species of plants and animals are disappearing from our earth virtually every day—irretrievably lost. The warnings of scientists are morally compelling to many of us, and it seems logical they might incite action on behalf of conserving our natural resources. But in my experience nothing shuts down students faster than the doom and gloom speeches I have made about our planet's health. They seem to inspire guilt, to make students feel overwhelmed, and at best to appeal to their minds, not necessarily their hearts and souls. But we educators are human, and those of us who care about protecting the earth are worried that others do not understand the urgency of our charge. Time and again children have taught me that our desire to incite students to act on behalf of the planet is best served by nurturing a sense of wonder and a deep relationship between each individual and any single place on this earth of his or her choosing.

Sheldon Berman, author of *Children's Social Consciousness and the Development of Social Responsibility*, looked at research on activists and found that positive social action was "less about moral principles and more about the sense of self as connected to others and to the world as a whole." For children, Berman points out, making sense of the world and finding their place in that world, is a process. "Children, in essence, feel their way into the world. The degree of connectedness that they experience determines their sense of efficacy and their interest in participation." Furthermore, the studies in question point to "an additional motivator of activism: the need for a sense of meaning and a sense of place within the larger context."[4]

While most of the research that Berman and others who study moral development cite deals most explicitly with the social domain, surely children's sense of connection to the earth and other living creatures is a factor in this search for meaning and a growing sense of self as part of a larger context. By nurturing such spiritual connections to the earth in children, we lay the groundwork for higher levels of moral reasoning and action. As educator Dave Mayo-Smith once pointed out to me, it's one thing for a child to want to save the rain forest because of its medicinal potentials, it's another for him or her to want to save it because it has its own intrinsic worth and value as a living entity. Mitchell Thomashow considers this shift in thinking fundamental to what he calls our "ecological identity" and describes a process of development in our awareness of our basic connection to nature. The rain forest must be valued and conserved because it is the lungs of the earth (in that it supports our atmosphere by producing oxygen and taking up carbon dioxide from the system). The rain forest supports and sustains us—it is a part of us.

Berman comments further that "as the level of moral reasoning increases, people become more concerned with their integrity and act in ways that are consistent with their beliefs." The integrating effects of being in nature—coming into wholeness—can lead to direct action. Every year, the students in Ocean Matters are required to design and execute a group research project. While this effort could focus on any topic of interest to the students, each year the group has decided to contribute to a monitoring project to assess the health of the reef. Students have then shared their data and made recommendations to the Caymanian Department of the Environment (DOE) for sustaining the health of the reef as related to managing diving pressures. The presentation of their findings to the DOE is voluntary, yet fully 90 percent of the students choose to participate, giving up their last days in paradise, which otherwise would be carefree. The passion our students have had for this project never ceases to amaze us. For Tayla, who volunteered to be group leader for this project one year, the experience carried an important "take home" message:

> I think back to the last couple of days [of the program], when we were putting together our research report, doing standard deviations, working really hard. We wouldn't have accomplished as much if we didn't all feel that way about the reef and care about the project and the topic. I have a quotation that sums it up, "Nothing in the world is accomplished without passion."

The Role of the Teacher

> I am alarmed when it happens that I have walked a mile into the woods bodily, without getting there in spirit. —Henry David Thoreau

Taking young people into nature does not guarantee a spiritual experience for them. One year in the Caribbean we had an unfortunate combination of two new faculty members who were not in tune philosophically with the program, two separate campuses (one for boys and one for girls), and a two-hour round-trip drive to our dive site. While some students claimed to have had a profound experience that year, for the majority of us—staff included—things never really "gelled." The faculty was busy putting out fires and dealing with logistics. The kids were fractured and distracted. There was little sense of community. The shift to a more dynamic, passionate learning environment never quite happened. A few times we could almost hear the gears shifting and sputtering, but like a car with a busted transmission we were stuck in second gear. We went home disheartened but more focused. Our failures that summer made us realize that part of the magic we had experienced in the past had something to do with the sense of community we were nurturing and our own passion and authenticity as teachers. So what then *is* our role as teachers?

Chris Gawle and I learned the answer to this question the hard way. After our first successful year with the program, we had approached our teaching with a very strong attachment to outcomes. We wanted the next year's students to care as much about the reef as the first group had done. We wanted them to do a research project that had a conservation bent. We wanted to change their lives. In our very first class that second year, Chris presented a compelling argument that our seas were in serious danger due to human activity, and that this threat, through shifts in weather patterns, could seriously affect life as we know it on our planet. Later we repeatedly asserted our wish that students do a research project that dealt with conservation. Our good intentions backfired. The students seemed angry with us, splintered as a group about which research topic to pursue, and uninterested about the threats to the reef. Truth be told, Chris and I were becoming disappointed in them and they could sense it. Out of sheer frustration, Chris and I stopped trying to influence their feelings and values. We were both surprised at the result. Slowly the group self-organized. Over the coming weeks, the passion we had sought to develop too early quietly emerged on its own. We had been arrogant and overbearing in imposing our own values on our students; given a break from our agendas, they developed their own, and the group did, in fact, eventually design a conservation-focused research project.

Paulo Freire calls this attachment to outcomes the "banking" model, wherein education becomes "an act of depositing" in which the students are the depositories and the teacher is the depositor. Freire furthermore called this model one of oppression, since the learners are seen as having a deficit.[5] When we let go of our agendas, however, we communicate our respect for the learner. This does not mean that we should not hold high expectations for our students. Demanding excellence is appropriate. Expecting a particular values transformation is not. The questions students seek to answer should be their own; the learning should be student-centered.

While such a constructivist approach is at the center of all good teaching, it is especially critical to inviting soul into an experience. Our souls are like wild animals, crouching in the shadows. We can stalk the animal and risk sending it running for deeper cover, or we can sit and wait and yield to its intentions, bearing witness to its presence. Most simply put, our role as teachers is to provide opportunities for students to authentically engage with nature so that, in the words of Rachel Carson, we nurture in children "a sense of wonder so indestructible it will last a lifetime."

An Ecological Pedagogy

The good news is that you do not have to take children scuba diving in the Caribbean to inspire this sense of wonder and connection. Students can develop a deep relationship with nature in their own backyards, whether they live in the city or the country. In fact, helping students connect to their own home places is preferable to taking them on exotic wilderness trips, which carries the danger that once the experience is over its more profound effects wear off. A relationship with a place in nature is like any good relationship. It should unfold over time, moving toward intimacy and respect. The relationship should not be one of dominance—the goal is "power with" not "power over." If we carefully support this process, children will come to know details about their places in the same spirit as an artist might study the face of one he loves. They will come to know the places' strengths and vulnerabilities.

Most classroom and enrichment programs in environmental education are thought of as science course work. This is one way we justify their place in the academic schedule: science is part of the core curriculum. But perhaps this alignment with science education has needlessly limited the quality of the experience of nature we provide for children. Science is a rational domain. It deals with facts, not feelings or intuition. Conversely, most outdoor adventure education focuses on feelings and inner process, not facts. In the Ocean Matters program, we have found that the most successful approach integrates both. While the content we teach is college-level marine biology, the methodologies we use to teach it combine art, literature, ritual, and other tools used in the practice of many of our world's religious traditions.

Here are some important considerations for any program aimed at developing children's sense of place and connection to the natural world.

BRINGING CHILDREN OUTDOORS

This might seem obvious, yet increasingly the majority of opportunities for children to learn about nature are vicarious: textbooks, nature TV, videos, and online projects. Many of these experiences are compelling. Via the internet, children can follow the migration path of a whale, for example, analyzing daily postings from a naturalist and sharing in the creation of hypotheses about the life history of whales. But while all of these exciting technological possibilities have value in teaching children about nature, to truly engage children's spirits you have to bring them outside.

It is helpful to plan outdoor expeditions and field trips to be what Kasha called "heads-under" experiences—ones that require students to engage directly with nature. As a supplement to the outdoors experience videos and other resources can help 1) to inspire wonder and curiosity, 2) to build up on students' questions with germane facts, and 3) to complicate and deepen children's thinking by providing information that puts their thinking in conflict. (See "Putting Feelings First," below, for information about the use of supplemental resources.)

CHOOSING A PLACE

As naturalist Richard Nelson writes, "There may be more to learn by climbing the same mountain a hundred times than by climbing a hundred different mountains."[6]

Together with your students, choose one place near your school and come to know it very well. The place you choose should have enough ecological integrity to be sufficiently complex for a study. That is, it should be relatively wild. The scale of the place can be large or small, depending on the age of your students, your access to nature, and the prior experience your students have had outside. There are two general rules of thumb I've discovered for this selection: 1) the younger your students are, the smaller the scale should be for your study (the older your students, the larger the scale); 2) with increasing experience in nature, students will be engaged by increasingly more detailed study.

Elementary school students will likely be engaged by a small patch of earth in your school's backyard. They can be absorbed for long stretches of time by digging for worms and insects and looking under rocks and logs—a natural treasure hunt. Adolescents will usually need larger tracts of nature to be sufficiently engaged. If this is the first time you and your middle or high school students have done such a study, you might choose an acre or more of forest or desert, for example, or a streambed or stretch of rocky shore. As your students gain more experience as a group, you might encourage them to become progressively more focused in terms of scale. They might eventually even choose one single tree to explore.

If you are limited to an urban location, do not be discouraged. Much can be gained from studying a small stand of trees in a city park or in your schoolyard, or from studying the moon and the stars regardless of your students' age and level of experience.

STUDYING ONE PLACE OVER TIME

You cannot really know a place until you've studied it over time. It's best if your study spans different seasons, different weather, different times of day. Remember that the span of time that is optimal is almost always eco-dependent. It is important to study a temperate zone ecosystem over four seasons, while in a tropical zone a shorter time scale may be appropriate. If you are exploring a small stand of forest in New England, for example, it would be best if you could study it throughout the year, but much can be learned about a coral reef within shorter time frames—daylight versus night, before or after storms. Aim to maximize the length of your exploration to capture the variety that is inherent to your ecosystem within the limits presented by your situation.

ENGAGING THE SENSES

Little in the way of traditional education engages all our five senses, but nowhere is this more important (and more possible) than out of doors. Throughout children's experience in nature, call upon them to use each of their senses. The goal is to help children develop a mindful presence outside—that is, to become aware of their surroundings at a level of detail that transcends our normally relatively detached way of being in the world. The goal is that they come to know a place through their bodies, not just their minds.

Focusing on one sense at a time can be a very useful way to do this. You might have students form pairs, close their eyes, and listen to their place, taking turns writing down everything their partner hears or any pictures or thoughts that come to mind. Or ask them to compare two branches of two different trees through touch or smell, or to pay attention to the sounds of birds or animals at different times of day or different seasons.

While most people are accustomed to learning about nature through visual observation, there are ways of seeing that go beyond students' usual experience. I was once on a ferry in Alaska when I heard a fellow passenger make note of how disappointed she was that she hadn't yet seen any whales on the trip, whereas I had seen many. I started to point out various whale signs to her and then to others who gradually gathered. Astounded, a woman asked, "How do you find them?" I had learned from two summers teaching on a whalewatch to see the telltale clear patch of water above where the animal has descended or the spray of their blow or the disturbance of their bait on the surface and the birds that might gather there.

One effective way to shift students' focus to such details is to have them walk through a very small stretch of nature taking note of everything they see. Through multiple passes on the same strip, they will start to notice different and new things. With excitement they can watch their list grow to incorporate the tracks of animals, their scat, a broken branch, bushes that have been mostly stripped of berries by birds, and so on. Later you might encourage students to hypothesize about what animal left the tracks or broke the branch, filling in valuable information as your students' questions require. Or you can encourage students to see nature more three dimensionally, by having them walk in silence paying attention to the shadows rather than the sunlit world. While I've often taken students on guided tours in nature, where *I* point out the interesting things we pass, I've found this is most effective when timed later in your time together; students' first several lessons on "seeing" should be solo.

PUTTING FEELINGS FIRST

Rachel Carson once wrote, "I sincerely believe that for the child . . . it is not half so important to *know* as to *feel*. If facts are the seeds that later produce knowledge and wisdom, then the emotions and the impressions of the senses are the fertile soil in which the seeds must grow." In our rush to meet academic standards, this simple wisdom is often sadly lost. Your first sessions with children in nature might predominantly explore children's feelings about the experience. The feelings then become the hook on which children's curiosity and desire to know more are hung. Later sessions in nature that are more content driven can likewise have a feelings component, though it need not be dominant. This is sometimes as simple as giving children time to reflect in journals or share with a partner how the experience has made them feel. Or it might involve responding to a piece of literature someone else has written about the ecosystem you are studying. Most importantly, it involves slowing down the experience enough to leave room for children's feelings and to show you value them by listening.

TEACHING THE FACTS

While the latest educational reforms have rightfully encouraged a quality of knowing that is deeper than rote memory, much has been lost, I believe, in our modern rejection of the discipline of memorization. When we memorize, we literally *re-member*, or again incorporate a distinct part into the whole, "adding it unto ourselves forever," as writer Brenda Ueland once described it. Students in the Ocean Matters program become proficient in identifying over a hundred reef flora and fauna—learning the Latin species names for invertebrates and algae that at first glance look like little more than "snot on rock" (as one teenager put it), as well as the common names for the more compelling reef vertebrates including fish, turtles, and sharks. While most students groan at first at the brute work involved in memorizing names like *Acapora palmata* and *Siderastria sideria,* I've yet to see a single one fail to eventually master this task given enough practice and support. And, most importantly, I've yet to see a student not moved by the sense of power and mastery that knowing the names of things imparts.

When we help students learn the names of the plants and animals that inhabit a place, we are helping them establish an intimate relationship with that place. Not to do so would be like setting students loose in a new school but suggesting they not learn the names of all of their new friends.

INCLUDING UNSTRUCTURED TIME

Many of us have special memories of playing in nature as children—climbing trees, inventing games, or simply playing hide-and-seek in the backyard. Unfortunately, these experiences are rare for many of today's children. When children "muck about" outside, they are developing their relationship with nature on their own terms. This is critical to both children's construction of meaning and their own sense of authenticity about that experience. Every moment that children spend in nature, even moments that seem silly and undirected to our adult eyes, can contribute to their growing sense of self and relationship with place.

AVOIDING SHAME OR GUILT

Once, early on in our work in the Caribbean, a small group of students spotted a green turtle on the reef while we were diving. In their excitement, several took off swimming in hot pursuit of the animal, and one eventually gained enough ground to touch its shell. The turtle looked back for one second and then hightailed it out of there. Green turtles are endangered and as such are protected by the Endangered Species Act, which clearly stipulates that such pursuit of an animal is illegal. That day, in our anger and self-righteous zeal, Chris and I followed the students out of the water, interrupting their squeals of excitement over the turtle sighting to lecture them harshly on why what they had done was wrong. I'll never forget their crestfallen faces— though at the time I thought I had done the right thing. Later that very same year I attended a conference at which nature writer Robert Finch described a similar experience with an enthusiastic child who had grabbed for an alewife during the annual run. My face became hot with recognition as Finch talked about how we adults often stamp out children's zeal with our admonitions, when in fact we should encourage their sense of wonder. I now handle such situations differently.

When a student does something clumsy or potentially harmful to a creature, it's most often out of excitement or ignorance. Rather than shaming students, we can first connect to and validate their enthusiasm and then invite them to take a larger perspective by asking what they think that creature might have been feeling at the time; most often they will make the commitment on their own never again to remove a creature from its home or to chase it or otherwise seek to possess it.

PROMOTING INDIVIDUAL AWARENESS
AND GROUP INTERDEPENDENCE

From literature and personal experience we know that times of solitude are often when people feel closest to nature, but leaving time and opportunity for solitude in an educational program can be difficult. I've found that cultivating even short breaks when students can be alone in nature works well, especially if the breaks are regular. Given unstructured time in nature, many students will spontaneously seek out solitude. It was common for students in Ocean Matters to sit alone on the rocks and gaze at the water or watch the sunset, or to sit under a tree by themselves during the free time we built into each day.

Equally important is creating a sense of a community through shared experience. The collective memory of a group's time in nature can help bridge differences among group members and create common ground. Interestingly, when we polled former students of Ocean Matters about their most powerful memories from the program, most from a given year shared the same story. The spotting of an eagle ray or the experience of a night dive can become almost a signature moment, creating a group identity.

These communal experiences are most profound, I've found, when they require students to be dependent on one another in some important way. In our group research projects, for example, each student had an essential role, and because each project was carried out on scuba, students took responsibility for one another's lives. As Kasha pointed out, such a connection is not left to chance: "I gained a trust in others out of necessity." It is important to set students up for success by supporting them in learning the skills of collaboration—communication, appreciation of differences, and the healthy expression of feelings. We used team-building activities throughout the program and held daily student-led research meetings to help deal effectively with any conflicts as they occurred.

USING RITUAL, MYTH, ART, AND REFLECTION

Art, myth, and literature are wonderful ways to connect to students' imaginations, to move from the particulars of their experiences to the universal. In Ocean Matters we have students draw each of the reef creatures they sight in a special notebook. While most of us are not particularly gifted artists, everyone seems to enjoy drawing, especially once any expectation about "talent" is removed. The simple task of drawing a creature creates a certain type of intimacy with that animal; the partnership of hand and eye concentrates one's focus on its shape and coloring and other important details. You might use a poem, an essay, or a folktale as a point of departure, or have children create their own stories and myths to explain phenomena in nature. Such activities stimulate children's imaginations and connect to a more universal level of experience.

Rituals honor the mystery inherent in nature and are useful team-building components if their symbolism is appropriate to your purpose. For example, you might try adopting the practice of using a "talking stick" to indicate whose turn it is to speak. The speaker's words are like the sound of the wind through the leaves—we only hear them if we really stop to listen. Likewise, the listener might hold a stone, to ground him and imbue him with patience. You might encourage students to create their own rituals or suggest some yourself.

WEAVING NATURAL METAPHORS AND OBSERVATIONS INTO CHILDREN'S LIVES

Even during your time with children indoors, nature can be a powerful tool for creating meaning. Nature's rhythms—the seasons, light and darkness, weather—can be apt metaphors for change in children's lives, just as they were for Dave. Just noting the phase of the moon as we might ordinarily note the date of the month can help shift students into a sense of groundedness and connection with nature; so can being conscious of the foods that are in season, or teaching children to tell time at night by looking at the sky, using the Big Dipper's position like the hands of a clock. Aim to present the natural world to be as significant as the man-made world by your conscious inclusion of it in your language and in your students' awareness.

NURTURING A SENSE OF PLACE

What's special about where you live? How did natural resources inform the culture of your area—the industry, the placement of homes? Do any of your roads follow older footpaths or livestock paths to natural resources such as water? What can the place names used by the native people tell us about the area that you didn't already know? How might using those names versus the Anglo names change your relationship to that place, if at all? What would the land look like if you stripped away all the development?

Few children (or adults) are aware of just how their towns or cities were shaped by nature. Boulders that they walk by every day may have been left by glaciers; the shape of a stand of trees on a hill might make the pattern of wind in that area visible. But they will not be likely to notice these things unless you encourage them to do so. Help children to form questions about their natural heritage and then do research. When answers are not available, encourage them to make their own best guesses. For example, if you cannot recover native people's place names for your area, have children create their own, honoring the special gifts of nature, like "place of eel fishing" or "place of river rocks." Special occurrences in nature, such as eclipses, storms, and migrations, can also be brought to children's awareness in order to better acquaint them with where and when they live.

The Power of Love

It is the day Chris is leaving early from the Caribbean to return home for his graduate school exams. I rush to class just in time to see him say good-bye to the Ocean Matters students. Chris has written on the white board in the classroom, "Take-Home Lesson: Replace the love of power with the power of love." The students consider it and several bow to write in their notebooks. Then, wordlessly, one by one, they get up and come forward to hug him. At six feet two inches, Chris has to bend to embrace the students. Individually each student is added to the hug until they are all enfolded into one complete unit.

Someone grabs my hand and I, too, am added to the heaping hug. A few shed tears. And then Chris is off in the van to the airport. Later I notice that one student, Helen, has changed the screen saver of her computer; it now flashes "replace the love of power with the power of love" as it sits on a common table near where we all are eating together.

Could it be that simple, I wonder? We've certainly learned a lot about love in our time together on the reef. Two years after we were all together with Jake, students from that year are still asking me about him and how he is doing. I've had to answer that I don't know. Jake's mother hasn't been able to give me any information about him; they have fallen out of touch. It's unsettling not to know where Jake is or if he's okay. I hope that he still has places where he feels he belongs, where he's not alone and his many gifts are valued. And I hope that if Jake calls out, he can hear the earth answer.

ZEPHRYN CONTE

The Gift of the Arts

I was standing in the wings for the very first time. It was en-
chanting. My eyes bulged as I strained to see across the brightly lit
stage, where off in the distance I could make out the small, attentive
faces of the audience. Intense heat pressed down from the lights, and I
remember noticing beads of perspiration flying off the dancers.
Everything on stage vibrated and shimmered—a super-ordinary
world that strangely reflected the architecture of my own imagination. I heard the audience laugh and suddenly I felt connected to
them, determined to do my best. Even at the age of five, I understood
that I was about to step onto "sacred ground."

It was our turn now. As I imagined the dance, I could feel my excitement about being able to communicate in this new way. Speaking
through movement felt intrinsic and timeless, so much more eloquent
than words. As we moved to the edge of the light, an awareness filled
my spirit. I was moving across a bridge—one I recognize now as the
bridge between my inner life of feelings and imagination and my
outer life of expression and form. The familiar strains of music beck-
oned, and with all of the time-worn rituals, months of practice, and
painstaking preparations coalescing to support me, I extended my leg
and stepped triumphantly onto the stage!

Art and Life

Artistic experiences can be deeply resonant and influential in the lives of children. They tap into children's innate creativity and give them access to symbolic languages, meta-languages, through which their unique and authentic voices can be heard. Indeed, my own memories of early artistic experiences remain as alive as if the events had occurred yesterday. They have inspired a love and respect for the arts that has guided a lifelong journey.

For many of the children with whom I have struggled, taught, and learned, the gift of the arts has sometimes meant the difference between safety or violence, emotional clarity or disturbance, school success or failure, belonging or isolation, hope or despair. Even after thirty years of teaching in diverse settings throughout the country, I am still awed by the power of the arts to nurture human beings and provide transformational, community-enhancing experiences. I have witnessed many young *and* adult learners experience personal or social growth through the "artistic process." Because of this, I no longer question if, rather I question why and how the arts can nurture the inner lives of human beings, build bridges between a person's inner experience and his or her external world, and build and strengthen community.

Understanding and refining methodologies that might enable everyone to draw insight and learning from the arts is a major educational challenge. If we view learning as creativity, invention, and experimentation, however, one might venture to say that the arts have always been at the center of the learning process. I believe that creativity is intrinsic to the human experience and that this is why the arts remain at the center of cultural rituals and rites of passage. And I often wonder, If *all* children were given the gift of the arts to fully explore their inner lives and develop their authentic voices, what would our communities be like and how would our culture change?

An Inner Journey

My introduction to Tara took place on her first day in my class, when she started a fistfight with another student. I was a performing arts teacher in the New York City public schools, where I specialized in developing a number of arts-in-general-education programs. Tara was one of my seventh graders at an alternative middle school that offered ongoing education in the arts as a regular part of every child's academic experience.

My students varied widely in their abilities and interest in performing arts, but Tara was exceptional for many reasons. In researching her background, I learned that she lived in a group home. She had been abused and abandoned by her parents, and on top of these emotional hurts, she had sustained physical injuries that rendered her partially deaf in both ears. She came to my class in the middle of the school year, when we were involved in a "movement unit."

After breaking up the fight on that first day, I gently invited Tara to "join the action" whenever she felt ready. At first she would not move her body or participate in any activities. She just watched. This behavior went on for several weeks. Her everyday movements were static and disconnected, and her kinesthetic relationship to her surroundings and to other people was stiff and awkward. This did not surprise me, given all that she had been through.

The challenge with Tara was how to invite her into the process of self-discovery that I believed could meet some of her most basic human needs. As Dr. William Glasser writes in his exposition of "control theory,"[1] all of our behavior is purposeful, and the purpose is always to attempt to satisfy basic needs that are built into our genetic structure. Tara's needs for power, belonging, freedom, and fun—Glasser's framework, which I have found very useful—had not been met successfully in her early life. Unmet needs very often underlie the feelings that are currently visible. Because arts activities promote pleasurable participation, cooperation, choice, and freedom of expression, I was hopeful that Tara's first performing arts class would help her address those feelings.

One day Tara startled me into the further realization that artistic environments and the creative spirit in which arts activities unfold can create a zone of safety for children that we are not always aware of. She helped me learn that they possess a calming effect that is particularly powerful for children who do not have regular exposure to centering experiences. In fact, many of my students have equated their artistic experiences with "feeling peaceful."

My students always wrote journal entries in a learning log, and while Tara had not been dancing with the class, she had always written in her log. My code of honor with students stipulated that if they did not want me to see something very private they had written, they could fold the page over and I would not read it. When I looked at Tara's log for the first time, none of the pages were folded, which was encouraging. There were many pictures and doodles from earlier days, but for her most recent entry she wrote,

> I feel very good in here today. I don't know why but I do. This room makes me feel good. I like to watch kids move. Some look funny. I don't ever feel this good in other places. Maybe there's some sort of psychic balance in here that makes people feel and see.

You can imagine my surprise at reading these sensitive words. Tara piqued my desire to reinforce the safety she had alluded to in her journal entry. Her reference to "feeling" two times, and her awareness of the concept of "psychic balance" were intriguing doorways that I wanted to keep open. Since journal writing seemed to be the safest medium for her, we began a journal dialogue. In this way, Tara could stay in the private and safe world of her journal, where she felt safe, while having the benefit of a pen pal. I wanted her to feel in control of the process.

THE ARTS AND EMOTIONS

The arts play a meaningful role in social and emotional learning and health. Creative arts experiences often provide expressive opportunities that give voice to emotional material that may be inaccessible through words. Artistic experiences often draw out feelings and awareness in unexpected ways. Tara's journal entry strongly reflected that. Even as an observer, she had received personal insights from connecting to the positive energy surrounding her.

An artistic form separates the creator from the creation. This can foster emotional learning in nonthreatening and even metaphorical ways. I was hoping that in time Tara's sense of safety would increase as she continued to watch the class's processes of performance, observation, and analysis. I also hoped she would come to see her classmates learning about themselves from our friendly analysis of their art. Art forms create a "buffer," allowing emotional privacy while increasing learning through the self-reflection, observation, and comparisons that occur organically as part of the process. The journal created an additional buffer for Tara, one I wanted to honor. She was obviously quite capable of learning from her observations, and the journal allowed her to be in control, which created emotional safety.

During the weeks that followed, Tara and I "discussed" a number of things in journal exchanges. I never pushed her to dance, although I would always ask her in class if she was ready. She would shake her head no. I wanted to learn more about why she liked to draw, so I asked her. This was her response:

> When I make a drawing, it's as if I am in my own safe world where nothing can affect me. I just go into this place where I calm right down and nothing else matters, at least then. I have too many feelings . . . they don't come out . . . I can't say things.

The connections between the emotions, the senses, learning, memory, and creativity become dramatically apparent in creative arts settings. Tara's making the connection to her unexpressed emotions, the effects of observing her classmates dance, and the journal writing were all gradually contributing to the social and emotional growth that was a byproduct of her performing arts experience.

THE ARTS AND PLAY

We were still doing our dance unit when one day I decided to conduct an experiment with learning through play. I had a hunch from something that Tara had mentioned in her learning log that playing a game might enable her to join us in movement.

For young children, play is a way to create security, to practice making meaning. The arts have an organic link to play in that many creative activities are play-like, or feel like play, because they are accessing imagination. Tara had been deprived of a safe play world as a young child, which had seriously affected her psychological, intellectual, and even spiritual foundations. Like many children in similar situations, she now turned to any creative forms available, instinctually, as a tool for emotional survival. I felt that her "doodling" had been just such a survival tool. When children create a piece of art, it validates their existence. Very often children "make art" as gifts for their loved ones. What they are giving is the gift of their creative spirit.

That morning I suggested that we play "Run, Stop, and Shape." Students were to create a motor movement, followed by a frozen shape, followed by a melting motion that needed to blend into someone else's shape. I made eye contact with Tara, giving her my usual look of "Are you ready yet?" She walked over to the rest of the group very calmly. I was waiting for her to sit down at any moment during the game, but she didn't. As she moved through each segment her smile appeared for the first time. Although her movements were awkward, she was taking a risk that everyone in the room realized was a big step. I had tears in my eyes. But what was especially remarkable for me was what happened with her classmates. Because everyone knew about Tara's difficulties, they were as surprised and pleased as I was with her success. Playing had opened a door for Tara, and when she chose to step through it the class demonstrated tremendous empathy and caring.

As the months followed, Tara slowly became more active with the class. She felt safer, to a point where she was able to express her emotions within the group. Her body softened and her movements became more fluid. Her hearing even seemed to improve as a result of some of the music listening activities we practiced. A child who had begun angry and withdrawn was now more trusting and open.

The Arts: Bridging the Internal and External Environments

> When words are no longer adequate, when our passion is greater than we are able to express in a usual manner, people turn to art. Some people go to the canvas and paint; some stand up and dance. But we all go beyond our normal means of communicating, and this is the common human experience for all people on this planet. —Murray Sidlin, former conductor of the New Haven Symphony

Tara's evolution from a hopeless and hurt child into a curious and playful one illustrates beautifully how education in the arts enhances learning by inviting discovery. Arts activities tend to draw learners in because they often engage or activate "felt-sense." By offering Tara creative experiences that made her feel something, along with opportunities to use her body and senses in directly manipulating color, shape, music, rhythm, or movement, this arts course was actually giving her a chance to practice crucial problem-solving skills. Because the arts shape self-discipline in contexts that tend to be creative and cooperative rather than competitive, students are provided with healthy opportunities to internalize and apply critical social and emotional skills. While the arts can be seen as technologies for increasing creativity, they also foster a healthy balance between the logical and creative functions of the brain. The gift of arts experiences is that they build the mental qualities or life skills of creative thinking, problem solving, self-reflection, perspective taking, empathy, resilience, effective communication, teamwork, and healthy risk taking.

In teacher trainings, when I introduce the idea of arts as communications technologies, I often say that each technology is like a culture, complete with its own rich history, language, and syntax. As with countries that have many states, regions, and dialects contained within them, a variety of arts traditions and forms exist within a larger domain of expression.

If you decide to study a particular art form, you'll learn its unique disciplines and techniques through traditions that reflect its history and culture. "Technique" is the vocabulary of each discipline, the means by which one learns to speak in the meta-language of a given form. I have always advocated that children have an opportunity to explore many different techniques or art forms in order to find the one, or the many, that resonate with their own needs and aesthetic sensibilities.

I often encourage non-arts teachers to use art experiences in their classrooms because this is sound educational practice. It allows children with different learning styles, capacities, and preferences to participate and provides diversified contexts within which to navigate. I love to see children "set free" in this way so that they can discover their intrinsic creativity at whatever technical level they have achieved and use it as a vehicle for exploration.

The list below summarizes a variety of artistic styles or traditions that exist within the larger domain of each form of creative expression:

- Writing/poetry—fiction, nonfiction, stories, essays, journals, interviews, dramatic scripts, song lyrics, rap, word art, therapy through written word expression
- Drama/theater—live theater in any setting, puppetry, circus, magic, traditional repertory, avant-garde, abstract and experimental theater, drama therapy
- Dance/movement—traditional forms of classical ballet; modern, theatrical, jazz, tap, character, hip-hop, ballroom, and ethnic dance; pantomime, martial arts, creative movement, movement as therapy
- Music/sound—classical European, "world music," American folk, bluegrass, blues, jazz, pop, hip-hop, spoken word, instrumental/vocal/percussion and body percussion, music as therapy
- Visual arts—painting, drawing, sculpture, pottery, scenery, architecture, film/video, photography, computer graphics, glassblowing, metal work, jewelry, costume and clothes design, visual art therapy
- Multi-media arts—a wide range of platforms and devices that bring together multiple art forms or media

Tools of the Imagination

> I think it is possible that the power of thought allows them [children] to create a place, not an imaginary place, but a place that is as real to them as reality. . . . During the time I'm writing, [a fictional place is] as real to me and as solid as this table top. I have smelled the smell of a campfire with an odor from no wood you'd ever have on earth. There has been quite a reality there. —Gene Roddenberry

This vicarious experience that Gene Roddenberry describes is an artistic tool for the imagination. It can put creativity in the service of learning by expanding students' perspectives, building empathy, and helping them with contextual clarity. In his creation of the famous TV series *Star Trek*, Roddenberry embodied the concept of vicarious expressiveness in a fictional invention called the holosuite. The trekkers were able to go into the suite (located on their starship), where they could holographically replicate people, objects, scenes, or experiences from any time or environment, and interact with them "for real." Or at least almost for real. Since the suite scenes were supposedly computer-generated, the characters "knew" that the experience only existed there, in the holosuite, yet when they were in the scene, it would seem to them as real as any reality.

By using vicarious expressiveness—the "holosuite" idea—many of my performing arts students have been able to gain a sense of contextual clarity about something of which they have no experiential knowledge. This is one way the performing arts can support other subjects, and a way arts-across-the-curriculum can work as part of an interdisciplinary approach. How can you know what a camel ride is like if you've never taken one? How can you know what it feels like to dive off a cliff if you've never stood on one? These are the questions that might inspire some library research and some vicarious expressiveness.

One year my seventh grade students were studying the redwood forests in science. In our performing arts class, I could reinforce their academic understanding of redwoods by artistically engaging them in activities that would join the subject with their creative imaginations. Instead of actually climbing a giant redwood tree, students researched and invented their own redwoods. They used different art forms to do this. Some drew, others used their bodies, others sang the song of the tree—in some cases they combined art forms. Having to engage and interact with the redwood in an artistic or metaphoric context brought that tree's texture, height, shape, location, and history vibrantly to life for the students. As one of my seventh grade performing arts students said in her journal,

> I feel this unit was complete and also educational in the sense of acting. The fun came through exercise, characterization, watching fellow classmates, and learning about voice and how to use it. The best part was personification. It's just being like an object, being free to say what you want. I feel this class helped me out.

Personifications is another drama activity I do with students that uses vicarious learning. It's a very lighthearted and pleasurable way to explore objects and ideas by assigning them human traits and allowing them to speak as if they had a consciousness. Not only does this activity provide great fun for the students (adults love it too), it has inspired some very insightful discussions about human feelings and needs. Another one of my eighth grade male students wrote in his learning log,

> Drama has taught me a lot. How to be many different characters. I can't wait till the performance next week. . . . Drama has changed me in a way, it has taught me to open up, show my feelings. It has also brought me closer to my friends. . . . I had fun doing personifications, giving human characteristics to a thing. It made me realize what a blender might think when it's mixing something.

Using your own vicarious abilities, imagine that you are walking into a beautiful theater. It is bustling with theatergoers, and you are very excited about the show you purchased orchestra seats to see. As you move down the aisle to your seat, you are preparing to suspend disbelief. For the next hour or so, you will most likely be practicing *believing*—believing for the moment that what you are seeing is true. Your belief will allow you to have a fuller experience of the play. It will allow you to feel more deeply and to connect your own experiences to the drama that you are witnessing on stage.

When we cry over a play, a movie, a book, or an inspiring piece of music, we experience an emotional catharsis made possible by suspending our disbelief, by opening ourselves to the vicarious experience of art. The suspension of disbelief happens almost spontaneously as the curtain rises in a theater. Like a child playing, we know how to immerse ourselves in the experience. If we were to watch the play only through a critical lens, we would be looking at what it *wasn't* instead of what it *was*. It is through our ability to suspend our disbelief that we gain access to information that might otherwise be hidden.

When students use the tools of imagination that are central to artistic and creative processes, they increase their mental capacities for related functions like elaboration (brainstorming), recognizing patterns, finding similarities, and developing empathy. These mental skills are important for collaboration and dialogue and greatly enhance students' abilities to develop positive relationships. Developing these skills in nonthreatening and enjoyable environments is one of the lasting gifts that the arts give learners.

The Creative Process

There is an interesting paradox that professional artists experience: they spend several years developing their technique in order to be able to forget it. Essentially this means that the techniques of one's chosen form become so imbedded and so fully mastered that one can speak and create through its meta-language with a freedom and abandon similar to that of an innocent child playing.

My experience with students continually reminds me that the creative spirit is intrinsic to us all, and that for many it has simply been "de-educated" by the time they reach adulthood. I can't tell you how many times I hear adults say things like "I can't draw" or "I have two left feet" or "I'm tone deaf." Hearing these comments makes me sad. Without art or music or dance or drama to connect us to our sensitivities and reflect our hopes and yearnings, the world would be an austere and robotic place. Everyone ought to be able to enjoy the experience of creating art. For some of us, though, finding the bridge between our inner lives and our outer world requires a map.

There are a number of ways that we could navigate or gain access to our creative impulses, but the one that I would recommend most widely is the writing process. Writing is not only a tool for self-discovery but a process through which other, different modes of communication can be understood more easily. Not only do I want my dancers, musicians, and actors to be artistically literate, I also want them to be meta-cognitive—to understand themselves as learners and performers. Journal writing is a natural vehicle for enhancing these understandings. The written word, and all of its syntactic and cognitive ramifications, can be used as the basis for the symbolic language of many different art forms.

In all of my performing arts classes, journal writing has been a very flexible tool for accessing creative ideas and sharing them with others. Journals can be valuable in any discipline, and they can be used in an integrated course of study. In my performing arts classes, the integrat-

ing element, central to each subject, has always been the creative process. Since each person's process is different, students' journals provided a framework for sharing the multiple experiences that ac-
company different phases of creating art. Creativity doesn't always
happen in a prescribed manner, and writing frequently helps capture
and facilitate the structure and sequence of each person's process. Using journals and verbally sharing the results with classmates seems to
be helpful to children and also works well with adults in a variety of
settings as a tool for problem solving.

Community and Individual Expression

The arts can also promote the kind of personal change that trans-
forms one's relation to community. For the last several years I've trav-
eled throughout the United States, giving workshops and visiting artists and community leaders who work with "at risk" youth in a variety
of community-based arts programs. Pat (a pseudonym) was a woman
of about thirty-two years, a mother of four, and very boisterous and
confrontational in her way of expressing her opinions during the
workshop she attended. The atmosphere of judgment that her comments created was stopping others from freely voicing their own, possibly quite different, opinions.

What was remarkable was the extent to which working in a range
of artistic mediums created deep and dramatic changes in this
woman. As we maneuvered our way first through large-scale drawing,
sound making, and expressive movement, and then through a variety
of journal and creative writing exercises, Pat's original hardness and
defensiveness began to melt and soften. Her perceptions of what was
happening—her "reality"—began to expand and shift. Her level of
tolerance and ability to listen to others increased with each activity. In
her own words, "The arts activities created an equality and freedom I
have never experienced in quite as safe and pleasurable a way." For Pat,
speaking through the meta-languages of art diffused the energy and
aggressiveness that had formerly come through her words, and gave
her alternative ways to express what was deeply meaningful to her.

At the end of the three-day workshop, she told me that the symbolic meanings embodied through the various art forms we had explored had spoken volumes to her. Because they allowed everyone, in-

cluding herself, to be more vulnerable, these creative experiences had enabled her to understand and value the contribution of each member of the community. The art itself had created powerful platforms for addressing the sometimes controversial issues we raised and discussed together, while the artistic meta-language and the spirit of playfulness allowed the group's verbal and even emotional defenses to drop enough for substantive problem solving to follow. Not only was Pat's perception of the community and her role and value in it transformed, her self-perception had grown as well. She wrote,

> You have facilitated the blending of my head, heart and body. . . . I now feel equipped to be a more productive member of this community I care so much about. . . . Also, I have added to my list of valuables—me.

Many students have reminded me through their own personal discoveries with movement, music, visual arts, or theater that the creative spark is indeed a part of every human being's heritage. Holding the arts central to education is an important part of nurturing people's inner lives. Even as adults I think we can recognize that when our own inner lives are nurtured it is easier to feel the empathy and compassion needed for building more positive, emotionally stable and culturally cohesive communities.

The arts can offer us pleasurable and even magical opportunities to explore ourselves and our world. They can transport us and teach us and enlarge our possibilities. At the end of the year, Tara wrote,

> In drama, and music and dance classes I've done things I never thought I could do. I know things about myself I never knew before. The best was the spatial studies, I could really feel it, my body never knew how to feel space before. . . .

JACOB NEEDLEMAN

Wendy, Sim, and Other Philosophers: High School and the Love of Wisdom

*W*hen I changed my major in college to philosophy, my father asked, "What do you *do* as a philosopher?" To which I replied, "I try to explore and confront the great questions of life." At a party given years later to celebrate my Ph.D., I overheard my mother jokingly telling a guest that I was "not the kind of doctor who does anybody any good." Yet my quest has been to meet the challenge of training the minds and nourishing the souls of students, being sure that when they asked for academic bread they were not given stones.

Our society has no place where the ultimate questions are honored as questions. Every institution and social form we have is devoted either to solving problems or to providing pleasure: the school, the family, the church, medicine, entertainment, our jobs. Even funerals are designed to comfort us rather than keep the question before us: You too will die—for what purpose have you lived? I like to ask my college students, "If you could ask only one question of the wisest person in the world, what would it be?" But most of the students have great difficulty voicing the questions of the heart. Our whole culture suffers from metaphysical repression, living without relationship to our metaphysical center.

Several years ago I received an invitation from the headmaster of a school near where I live. Would I be willing to speak to a class of high school students about philosophy? Distinguished guests from the local community were being asked to conduct small classes throughout the day. Students would choose from a smorgasbord of civic leaders, scientists, artists, journalists, and college teachers such as myself.

The fact that my own children had attended the school made it difficult for me to say no, which I ordinarily would have done. Speak to teenagers about philosophy? The thought terrified me. Twenty years of teaching college-age students had made me painfully aware of how difficult it is to discuss serious ideas in a way that does justice to both the academic needs of young people and the deeper wish for understanding that brings many of them to philosophy in the first place. How many times had I come to the end of a lecture or a whole course feeling I had closed more doors than I had opened? Well, with my university students, most of whom were in their twenties, I could always excuse myself a little. By the time they appeared in the university, many of them had already "shut down." God forbid that I should try to play the guru. In any case, at the very least I could help my college students experience the value of conceptual analysis and intellectual criticism. If, while questioning their own assumptions and beliefs, some of them could then glimpse the power of the great ideas we were studying, then perhaps I had done all that a professor of philosophy could do. Perhaps.

But teenagers? I remembered a little of what I was like at that age. I had most definitely not shut down. I believed in Truth and I believed in Answers. I needed to serve something higher than myself, and yet at the same time I yearned to establish my own personal ego.

There was one adolescent experience that only much later in my life did I understand. I remember it down to the smallest detail. I had just turned fourteen. It was a bright October afternoon and I was walking home from school. I remember the trees and the colored leaves underfoot. Suddenly my name, "Jerry," said itself in my mind. I stopped in my tracks. I whispered to myself, "I am." It was astonishing. "I exist." I began to walk again, but very slowly. And my existence was walking with me, inside me. I am fourteen years old and *I am.*

And that is all. I did not speak about this experience to anyone, for no other reason than that I gradually forgot about it. I went on reading every kind of book about the mind, nature, science, philosophy. I read great novels. I plunged into classical music. But not once did anything I read, or anyone or anything I heard, make mention, even remotely, of such an experience. Nothing in my environment or education reminded me of it. How could that be? What is culture, what is education, if it makes no place for that experience? And further, what is the right way of supporting such an experience without spoiling it by the wrong kind of talk?

Meanwhile, I had been fond of referring to philosophy as an awakener of the real, gut-level questions of life, and equally fond of complaining that students were not free to address these questions in educational institutions.

I consider the ten great questions of philosophy—and of life—to be the following:

- Are we alone in the universe?
- Who am I?
- Why do we suffer?
- Is death the end?
- What can we know?
- Why is there evil?
- What can we hope for?
- What ought we to do?
- How should we live?

The eleventh question is, What is love?

But what if someone actually asked one of these questions? Was I prepared for that?

On the morning of my talk I was as nervous as I had been when I first started teaching twenty years before. There they were, about fifteen boys and girls, and there I was—talking, talking, talking. I couldn't stop talking. Hands started waving in the air and I finally called on one of the students. But no sooner did she start to bring her question out than I steamrolled over it with an answer that left her absolutely no room for further questioning. I went on talking—engagingly, amusingly, animatedly, bringing in Plato's cave here, the Upanishads there, St. Augustine's concept of evil, Kierkegaard, Spinoza, Hegel...

Time flew by. The bell rang and suddenly the class was over. That was it, that was all. As the students cheerfully filed past me and as I smiled at each of them, exchanging a few informal remarks, I began to realize in my gut what had happened. To be precise: *nothing.* I remained behind in the empty classroom at the desk. A dense fog began to lift and images of young, open faces appeared before me. Then another bell rang and I heard a soft tapping at the glass door. The next class was due to start. The students had been waiting politely, and no doubt in puzzlement, for me to come out of the room.

In the days that followed, each time I thought of that fiasco it stopped me in my tracks. Gradually, but distinctly, I began to recognize by its "taste" a certain process taking place with respect to my own cherished views about philosophy and the education of young people. I myself was coming into question. I hadn't expected that. And now I am in New York breakfasting with an old friend who has become the director of a new philanthropic foundation. Am I planning any projects, he asks me, for which I would like to apply for support? To my astonishment, I find myself saying, with complete assurance in my voice, "What I'd really like to try is to teach a course in philosophy to teenagers."

Who was it who said, "Be careful what you ask for in life—you may get it"? In two weeks I began teaching philosophy at San Francisco University High School. The announcement bravely read as follows:

The Crisis of the Modern World (nondepartmental offering). Beyond the massive problems of the modern era—problems of natural resources, war, crime, the family, social justice—there lies a deep confusion about the meaning of human life itself. Who am I? Why was I born? What is the purpose of human life on earth? These questions have been asked since the beginning of time, but never have the answers been harder to search for than here at the end of the twentieth century. The aim of this course is to connect the real, concrete problems of the day with the universal questions of the ages.

In planning this course I thought about how I first became interested in ideas when I was young. What author first helped me? The answer surprised me: Bertrand Russell. I remember clearly the first time I read Russell. It was shortly after the start of my third year in high school. I sat by myself in some wooded area with a pile of books from the public library next to me. I picked up Russell's *Human Knowledge: Its Scope and Limits* and stayed glued to that book for the next three hours, even missing lunch. Why? What happened?

I couldn't follow much of Russell's sophisticated thought about science and human experience, so I didn't agree or disagree with his point of view. Something much more important and elemental was taking place in me. Russell spoke about human language and I realized that language *exists.* I spoke language, I read language; poetry and novels and books, and perhaps music and art were also language. He discussed space and time, and I realized that space is all around me, that everything exists in space, and that time flows everywhere, I am in it, everything is in it—but what is it? He wrote of ethics. My worries and problems, were they not ethics? And mind—I have mind and I have a body, and everything I see is a body, but where is the mind?

The loneliness I had been feeling dissolved; it simply dried up as the various aspects of myself were presented to me as objects of inquiry in the large world. I knew then that there exists something that one might call *clarity.* It was an entirely new feeling and yet, at the same time, strangely intimate and warm. Critics of the contemporary era often speak of the alienation and cosmic loneliness produced by the modern emphasis on the scientific attitude. They have their point, but it has no weight when placed against the first taste of objectivity toward oneself. There is nothing cold about this. On the contrary, my experience reading Russell was when I first began to feel that there is a home for humanity behind the appearances of this happy/unhappy world.

As I reflected on those early days, I realized that I had been worrying too much about the content of the course I was about to teach and not enough about the search that needs to be brought to all philosophy. I don't agree with Russell; I believe his vision of reality is shallow, that his concepts of human nature and knowledge lead nowhere. Yet his was a greater mind than my own, and once I needed to listen to it.

SEPTEMBER 10

There were fifteen students in my new class, exactly the right number. But before and after its first meeting I found myself wondering more about the students passing me in the hall who hadn't signed up. At their age, would I have risked taking such a course? Maybe not. There was one boy who particularly interested me, and I watched him for a few minutes. He was sitting by his locker amid a disorderly pile of books spread out on the floor. His head was buried in his new physics text and he was rapidly turning the pages, oblivious to what was going on around him. I went up to him.

"Can you tell me where Room Eleven is?" I said.

He looked up, startled. He could have been me: he had a round face, small features, and unkempt brown hair; his shirt hung out on one side of his trousers. "It's right over there, Professor," he said, pointing just down the corridor. So he knew who I was.

"Taking physics this term?" I said.

His eyes lit up. "Yes. I want to go into science. I wanted to take your course, but it's at the same time as physics."

It *was* me. I walked down the corridor, smiling about that boy. He had said, "I want to go into science," in the way an older person would have said, "I want to know, I want to understand."

But when he grew up would he recognize that his wish to understand was as much a part of his nature as his arms and legs or the color of his eyes? I am convinced that we are born with that wish implanted in the very tissues of our bodies. When does it stop sounding in so many of us? Is it possible to insert even one or two ideas in young people's minds that can come to their aid when life begins to do its job on them, to help them remember that wish and be moved by it, even unconsciously, toward a real search for truth?

At the beginning of my first class I talked briefly about the meaning of the word "philosophy." The students were far more nervous than I was. The assistant headmaster had told me that some of the brightest students in the school had signed up for the course; that partly explained their tension. Even one real idea, presented in a diffuse and simplified manner, can be frightening to a mind accustomed only to mastering concepts.

I asked them each to write down the one question they would put to someone really wise—a Moses or a Socrates or a Buddha. What came back were mostly cramped little fragments written in the margins of the paper or surrounded by immense white spaces:

"Is God real?"

"Why are we here?"

"Must there be a reason?"

"Where's it all going—the universe?"

"Why were we given a more advanced brain than other animals?"

I tucked the papers into my folder, promising to discuss all these questions later. But to myself I was making quite another promise. I would give them the same task in a month or so. By then they would not find it so strange to have to formulate "the questions of the heart." Not that they would find it easier—on the contrary. I promised myself they would be thinking about their question in almost every activity of their lives.

We were meeting three times a week for forty-five minutes at the end of the school day. I liked that arrangement. High school students are tired and fidgety by then, but this was outweighed by the fact that our class, coming last, would be the impression they took home with them. Their being tired is not so bad, I thought. Let them spend their mental attention on geometry or French or chemistry, where it really is needed; let them come to philosophy a little less interested in "figuring things out." Because if under those conditions they become interested, maybe it will be coming from a different place in them. I wanted them to be dreaming at night about philosophy.

As I expected, what really touched them were metaphysical and cosmological ideas. As an experiment, I started each class one week by discussing a problem of current concern: the ecological crisis, the threat of nuclear war, the problem of world poverty. I only wished I could have filmed their reactions to show the difference between the beginning and the end of each class. In the beginning, out came all their opinions and moral concerns—everyone talking at once, hands waving in the air, arguments, information from the latest newspaper article or TV show. Some of them were extremely well informed. We all played our parts, as though reading from a script entitled "Interesting Exchange about a Serious Issue." Because they were a little tired, however, and because they were not quite adults yet, their opinions had not yet become fully crystallized. In one moment, they were passionately denouncing some ecological crime and in the next they were giggling or just staring out the window.

But as soon as cosmological or metaphysical ideas were introduced into the discussion it was as though a magic wand had been waved. Fidgeting stopped. Wisecracking, interrupting, and talking over one another stopped. An attention that was quiet, open, and unforced appeared in the room.

For example, ecology. How to preserve our biological environment in a world addicted to its accelerated destruction? "Nations and people have to change their life-styles," said one student. Another argued for the development of "intermediate technology." The subject of whales and rain forests led one student to propose a sort of international task force and pressure group. This led to the idea of world government, which one student claimed was unrealistic. He was shouted down by others who argued that since it was now a matter of physical survival on the planet, the governments of the world could come together out of sheer self-interest. Yet another student who had been studying Native Americans spoke of "walking lightly on earth." This brought the whole discussion back to the problem of our relationship to nature.

At just that point I asked one of those questions that have become a sort of joke among sophisticated people but which, under certain circumstances, acquire the primordial power that they once had for almost all of us.

"What is a human being?"

Silence ensued. After a few seconds I added, "And why are we on earth?"

OCTOBER 1

I ended the class today by raising one of those philosophical problems most argued about: Is taking another human life ever justified? Usually this sort of issue is guaranteed to generate controversy—killing is wrong, but one has the right to self-defense, etc. Killing is wrong, but one must protect one's family, etc. Killing is wrong, but there are such things as just wars; for example, the war against Nazi Germany, etc. Such discussions invariably end with the conclusion that some form of world government is needed. And everyone goes home happy, even though suspecting down deep that nothing of the sort is ever going to take place. Everyone goes home also half-consciously aware that carefully defined distinctions between murder and socially justified killing are irrelevant to the question that lies behind the problem of war, the question of the real origins and meaning of violence.

"How can anyone ever decide whether killing is right or wrong?" said one student.

"What do you mean?" I said. He didn't answer.

"I know what he means," said another student, Lois, after an uncomfortable pause. All eyes turned to Lois, who hardly ever spoke in class.

"He means that if you hate someone you can't help yourself. You just want to kill them."

"That's right!" said the first student, whose name was Sim.

"How can you tell people not to hate other people?" Lois said. "Birds fly, fish swim, people hate."

"That's right, but people also love, don't they?" Sim said to Lois. Then he turned to me and asked, "What makes people hate or love?"

As I was about to say something, he cast his eyes down and gave out a long, low whistle. "You know what?" he said. "Are all the wars of human history just that—love and hate?" He whistled again in amazement. "Millions of people, bombs, terror, destruction, masses of people moving from place to place—Jesus! Is it all just emotions? The planet earth is floating in emotions!" Lights started going on in Sim's eyes.

On this note the class came to an end. I sat at my desk pretending to be gathering up papers, waiting to see who would want to speak privately to me. But everyone slowly filed out.

OCTOBER 8

Still no one has taken any sort of initiative, but I have decided on a simple method of getting to speak privately with each student without making it obvious why. I have put a dozen books on reserve in the school library and am requiring the students to choose one and write a report about it. I told them I would meet with each of them separately to judge which book would be best for them, but that meanwhile they should look over all of them. They all feel the demand to produce something—that is, they are relieved to see some structure emerging in the course. But some of them are now vaguely aware that our real aim has nothing to do with accomplishing anything. My task is to engage that part of them that needs to achieve while calling gently to the part that dreams of Truth. In the first half of my task I will have to be credible, believable—but not too believable. In the second half, I will have to be subtle, indirect—but not too subtle.

How can I, who am myself so rarely in contact with these two aspects of my own nature, presume to guide others in this realm? I brush aside these doubts. In the first place, there is no question here of guiding anyone. I myself am looking, seeking. Can I detect the difference in these young people between the love of wisdom and the need to function happily in the world around them? To see this difference in them, I must try to see it in myself as well. I discover again and again that the real questions of living, those which lie behind the world of appearances and problems, emerge out of this one fundamental question concerning my own two natures.

I keep thinking of those crabbed little formulations scrawled in the margins of those blank sheets of paper on the first day of class. In a year or two, I fear, even that will no longer be possible for most of them. These questions are educated out of most of us by the time we reach so-called maturity. I want my students to feel the natural right to ask of the universe those simple, gut-level questions that are most compelling in childhood, those that most often appear later only in moments of great disappointment or tragedy. One hears everywhere of rights—the right to life, the right to choose, to do what one wants with one's body. But there is a deeper right within human nature: the right to ask, Who am I? Why am I here? There are great answers to these questions but they do not appear until one has learned how to ask them with the whole of one's self.

A good friend of mine says I am "inculcating faith." I can accept that. It is not, however, faith *in* something. It is simply faith itself, without any object, without any awareness even, or self-consciousness. Faith I define as the deeply sensed permission to seek meaning. Amid all the beliefs of our era—belief in religion (rather than God), belief in science (rather than truth), belief in morality (rather than goodness)—what has been stifled and crushed is the faith that emanates from the essence of human nature. Down deep, we have been forbidden by fear and vanity to ask the questions of the heart. Thus we grow up settling for the answers of the ego.

OCTOBER 15

My first appointment today with Wendy helped me to understand something of critical importance.

Wendy is the only student in the class whom one might call troublesome. She often comes in late and is usually the chief culprit in launching the class into spasms of giggling and chattering. Her posture is almost always a profound and defiant slouch, eyes rolling ceilingward while the wisecracks and running commentary pour from her as from a horn of plenty. Involuntarily, I like her very much and I find she is a useful barometer. When Wendy is quiet, it's a sure sign that something real is happening in the class.

Because of Wendy I have already discovered something important about speaking seriously to young people. When a student in the class is restless, complaining, or chattering, my habit has been to interrupt my train of thought and try to bring the inattentive student back to the subject at hand. Just the other day, after having done that for the fifth or sixth time during the class period, I tried something else. Why, I asked myself, should my own attention always be drawn away by whichever member of the class happened, at a given moment, to be behaving the most outrageously? At a crucial moment in my presentation Wendy started making faces at the student in whose direction I was looking. That particular girl, a lively redhead named Heidi, averted her eyes from me, looked at Wendy, and returned to me with an embarrassed grin spread all over her face. I went on speaking in Heidi's direction, but as usual, all force drained out of what I was saying. For the first time, however, I was neatly struck by the absurdity of speaking about something serious into a silly adolescent face. Instead of trying to get the student interested, I simply passed my eyes to the student next to her, who happened to be Sim.

But this time even Sim, my "pet," was not paying good attention, and so I swiveled to the next student, and to the next, quickly and evenly surveying the whole class until I found a face with attention in it. It was this face I spoke to, while retaining some awareness of the restlessness of some of the other students. When, inevitably, the face I was speaking to began to lose its openness, I quietly moved on again, always directing myself to the face with the most feeling in it.

The results were excellent. Not only did my ideas develop in a normal sequence, but the emotions of the rambunctious students died down quickly and naturally. And the general level of the attention in the class remained rich in texture. The same thing happened right at the end of the class, again with Wendy, who was overcome by a sulking, impatient self-pity about something. Again, I resisted the impulse to get her out of it and concentrated on Sim, who by now had regained his usual expression of wonderment.

I promised myself to explore this approach fully in the future, both for what it could teach me about young people's wish for serious inquiry and the automatic forms of resistance to that wish, and also for what it could teach me about the agitated emotions that arise in myself and the unnecessary amount of attention I give them.

However, the challenge that emerged for me from today's class— learning to connect to and speak with the person behind the face— seems to be of overriding importance for the moment. And so here is Wendy standing by my desk clutching the Bhagavad Gita. She is wearing a pretty blue dress and lipstick, instead of her usual old jeans. Is it because of our appointment? Where to go to get to know her? I don't want the environment of the school to intrude, so I take her to a nice park about two blocks from the school to sit on a bench and talk. It's a typical October day in San Francisco: hot sun, clear air, everything green as spring.

"I see you've chosen one of the books," I say. She takes her copy of the Bhagavad Gita from her bag and handles it as though it were a block of wood. She thumbs the pages unconvincingly. I decide not to ask her why she has chosen that particular book because she has obviously not chosen it at all. She mumbles something about her interest in studying foreign cultures and says that in one of her classes last semester she did a report on an African dance troupe. She then purses her lips prettily and stops talking, waiting for me to get on with the interview.

I haven't the faintest idea how to go on. What have I gotten myself into? Somehow or other, I start the conversation again and soon find myself listening to descriptions of Wendy's older brother, her family's plans for the Christmas holidays, and her own plans to visit the East Coast colleges to which she is thinking of applying. I ask her what she considers the most important thing in her life and immediately feel like biting my tongue. I see the lies start to form in the expression of her face. Of course they do; she has no "most important thing" in her life—why should she? But it's too late. She fabricates something about wanting to be free from oppression yet self-controlled, or something like that. I have made her lie, or reinforced a lie in her.

Now she goes on, unreeling her "experiences," each more trivial—that is, adolescent—than the one before. Is it fair to say that? She confesses her heart's desire of wanting to travel through Europe on her own, "feeling the pulse of other cultures." She is watching me as closely as I am watching her and she is made uncomfortable by my unspoken reactions. I see this, and then pretend to be more interested in her experiences than I am. Inside, I am amazed by two things: the emptiness and artificiality of Wendy's personal world and my own prior ignorance of this fact. And yet I like her even more now than before. I look into her eyes and there is a person there. What is a person? Something raw, unformed, and tremendous; something intensely living and intelligent lies behind that smooth, rounded face. It has nothing whatever to do with her "experiences."

In that moment I understood something about education. Or, rather, I let go of something I had long believed in. I had always liked to think that, ideally, education means to bring something out that is already in the person, as opposed to stuffing something into the person—information, automatic manners, etc. What was to be led out (*educere*), I believed, was the knowledge or understanding that is contained as a seed in every human being. This view I have shared with many people, including professional educators who draw a sharp distinction between teaching necessary skills and information and this other more profound meaning of education.

After speaking to Wendy, I can no longer accept this distinction so simply. A teenager, she still wears her artificiality and lies like she wears her blue dress and lipstick—awkwardly, transparently. I see her in a year from now—no longer wobbling on her high heels, the lies she has been encouraged to tell about herself now carefully trimmed and fashioned to last a lifetime. She will become "interesting," that is, a good liar. She will begin to "find her identity," that formation which captures all her own psychic energy and which draws all the attention of those who meet her. Now I can still see the light of a person behind her face and I know she vaguely senses this light in herself. This division of attention in her and in my perception of her makes us both uncomfortable. This discomfort is the last, natural call in us of the question "Who am I?" just before it becomes covered over by the problem of "establishing one's identity."

I know now one undoubted fact about adolescence. It is a time when the question of the self is a natural companion, a light that soon flickers and goes out. Often, this is simply degraded under the term "self-consciousness," in its negative sense. No wonder the legends of adolescence are so strange to us: the power to see the mythic unicorn vanishes when innocence is lost. The unicorn is the person, the single one, the holy individual. To see the unicorn is to experience the question by sensing the person in "myself" alongside the social self in all its powerful unreality.

Yes, something has to be put into young people, but what? And how? What is the food of that light within them? How to speak to the personality so that the person also hears?

OCTOBER 22

Today it was Sim. I have been looking forward to this meeting for weeks. Something about Sim has attracted and intrigued me from the beginning. He is like a mariner who wants to inhabit every new land that comes into view. But today there is something troubling Sim and he is strangely reticent. Walking with him toward the park, I learn that there has been a death in the family—his grandmother. The funeral had been on the weekend; this is his first day back at school and it has been difficult for him.

The park is unusually crowded today. The playground area near the benches is filled with little children shouting and squealing. Sim and I find a place as far away from the bustle as possible. What is troubling Sim is not so much the death of his grandmother as the grieving of his father. His grandmother was apparently quite old, well into her nineties. She died suddenly, without any long illness or gradual decline, and so it was a great shock for the whole family on the morning that she failed to come down for breakfast. When Sim saw her in death, his first reaction was that this was not his grandmother lying there. As he tells it, the person in the bed was like a statue, a piece of stone. His grandmother, he felt, had simply gone away. He could not believe anything had died.

His father, usually so strong and capable, was apparently inconsolable. Sim had never seen anyone cry like that, or so often. His father would all of a sudden put his head down and his whole body would begin to shake convulsively. This could happen anywhere, any time. To Sim, this manifestation was more inexplicable than death itself.

In the midst of this account Sim asked, in a voice almost entirely free of emotion, "At the cemetery, when the coffin was being covered with earth, my father recited a prayer praising God, and I had to recite it, too. Why is that? I didn't feel like praising God for creating death. And my father was crying when he praised God. If you ask me, I think he must have been hating God at that moment." Then he said, "Dr. Needleman, why does death make people weak?" I could hardly believe my ears. I thought I knew all the kinds of questions people ask about death.

I turned away from Sim's wide-open face. Were there really any ideas or thoughts about death that were as deep as that question? Was I supposed to pretend that I was any stronger than Sim's father or anyone else? I found myself saying, "Real feeling is not weakness, Sim." The moment I said that, I understood something about the need for philosophy in the life of everyone, young or old. There are ideas that increase or deepen feeling, and there are ideas that draw us away from feeling. The subject of death must always be part of real philosophy— but in order to deepen the feeling, not in order to remove it.

"You know," I continued, "the ancient philosophers taught that the world we live in is impermanent and constantly changing. Always and everywhere there is birth and death, coming-into-being and passing-out-of-being. We've been talking about this in our discussions of Plato, do you remember?" Sim nodded.

"But Plato also spoke of something else that doesn't change," I said.

"You mean the eternal ideas—Good, Justice, Beauty . . . ," Sim began. I interrupted him.

"Think of them as laws of the universe. Everything changes, but the laws never change. Everything obeys fundamental laws. *Everything.*"

"Isn't that what science says, too?"

"Yes, but science has only discovered the laws of material objects. They haven't yet discovered the laws that govern life and death, nor the laws of the mind."

"Then," said Sim, "that means that death is not the strongest thing in the universe." I waited for him to complete his thought. "The laws are stronger. Even death has to obey the laws?

"I can understand," said Sim, "that death is necessary. Things have to die to make room for other things to be born. But why did it have to be that way? And . . . just because it's necessary, does that make it good? And . . . even if it is necessary and also good, how can the thing that is dying believe it is good? Nobody wants to die, do they? Animals never want to die. People never want to die, do they? I don't want to die, even if it *is* necessary."

I could not take my eyes from Sim's face. The division between the person and the thought had disappeared. Was I speaking to a question in the form of a person, or to a person in the form of a question? Sim did not have this answer; he was this question.

We were about to get up and leave, the sun was already touching the horizon, and Sim came back to his father's grief.

"Is there anything I can do to help him?" he asked.

"Yes," I said, "Don't automatically think of what your father is going through as a weakness. In other times and in other cultures the period of mourning was often considered very sacred and people would come to the mourner to receive his blessing, or to ask for his help. Suffering can bring wisdom and compassion."

"But how can that be?" he said. "People die all the time, all over the world. So, how come so few people have wisdom?"

"Try to find out what Plato says about that," I answered. "Suffering doesn't automatically bring wisdom. People have to want wisdom beforehand, otherwise it brings the opposite of wisdom. They have to want it very much. They have to learn how to look for it, how to inquire after it—that's what Socrates taught.

"What's the name that Plato gives to this desire, this love of wisdom?" I asked Sim, after a pause. Sim's face brightened. "Philosophy," he said, "but my father isn't a philosopher!" I laughed.

"Don't be so sure," I said. "A philosopher isn't just someone who reads books and takes courses."

Soul of Students, Soul of Teachers: Welcoming the Inner Life to School

*I*t is our first "senior honoring ceremony," designed to celebrate each graduating senior, not just the few who have shown out-standing achievement in academics or athletics. A cross section of the community—parents and faculty—is gathered in the chairs behind the students and teachers who will address them.

After a welcoming speech by the school principal, a teacher stands before a surprised and curious student.

"I have watched you grow this last year and become strong," the teacher says. "When you came into my class, I could tell that you were used to being one of the clowns. Yet when it came time to share our stories, you took the first risk. You inspired all of us with the courage of your vulnerability. I want to honor you for the warmth you brought to each one of us, and the initiative and courage you've shown. I re-spect you as a leader and value you as a friend."

The young man beams. His father behind him looks stunned. This is his younger son, the cut-up, the disappointment after the academic achiever who went before him. The one who has brought this father too many times to the disciplinary dean's office. Now, after listening to one of the most respected teachers in the school describe the outstanding gifts of character his boy has demonstrated in his final year of high school, the father's face begins to soften. Tears glisten. He places his hands on the broad shoulders of his son. One squeeze tells this boy that his father has heard, is willing to see him in a new light.

In the father's eyes looms perhaps the largest question of all: *What went right?* And the answer, though elusive, is quite simple. At the heart of every adolescent experience is an exquisite opening to spirit. An awakening of energy when larger questions of meaning and purpose, of ultimate beginnings and endings, begin to press with an urgency much too powerful to be dismissed as "hormones." What went right this year for this young man is that he found experiences that nourished his spiritual development. This secular school created a place for his soul, and he flourished.

Honoring soul in education means attending to the spiritual development of students. The body will not grow if it is not fed; the mind will not flourish unless it is stimulated and guided. And the spirit of the child will suffer if it is not nurtured. A soulful education embraces the many and diverse ways we can satisfy the spiritual hunger of today's youth. When guided to find constructive ways to express their spiritual energy, young people can find purpose in life, do better in school, strengthen ties to family and friends, and approach adult life with vitality and vision.

For many years it was considered dangerous for educators to address the question of spiritual development in schools. But after decades of headlines about "a generation at risk" we dare to do so: the void of spiritual guidance for teenagers is a contributing factor in the self-destructive and violent behavior plaguing our nation. For many young people, drugs, sex, gang violence, and even suicide may reflect a search for connection, mystery, and meaning as well as an escape from the pain of not having a genuine source of spiritual fulfillment.

Only in recent years—in response to persistent violence in our inner cities and schoolyard massacres in small towns and suburbs—are educators and social scientists beginning to acknowledge the enormity of this spiritual void. Professor James Garbarino, an expert on youth violence who teaches at Cornell University, speaks about "soul death" and the importance of kindling the "divine spark" in what he calls "lost boys." The day after the Columbine massacre, he asserted that "a very important part of all of this [is] the spiritual emptiness that so many kids feel . . . and when they feel it, when things go bad in their lives, there's nothing to fall back on and also there's no limits to their behavior." Over the last twenty years, my passion has been to understand how we can address this spiritual emptiness: *How can we nourish the soul at school without violating the separation of church and state or the deeply held convictions of families or teachers?*

This effort was inspired by two dimensions of my experience working with adolescents in the late seventies. I saw the persistent suffering that American teenagers cause themselves and others across the lines of class, race, and geography; I also saw that for many young people the search for meaning and purpose is a very lonely one. As I began to work with colleagues to create a safe place for students to ask their deepest questions, I witnessed an exquisite awakening to spiritual awareness, wisdom, and wonder.

Working with teams of educators around the country in both private and public school settings, I have created a curriculum, methodology, and teacher development program that can feed the awakening spirit of young people as part of school life. The Passages Program—a set of principles and practices for working with adolescents that integrates heart, spirit, and community with a strong academic component—is a response to what matters deeply for teenagers; their usually unspoken questions and concerns are at its center. When students participate in a curriculum that invites them to share what matters most to them, learning comes alive with connections that bring meaning, higher-order thinking skills, and motivation.

I first discovered this approach at the Crossroads School in Santa Monica, California, where I worked for seven years as chair of the department of human development, building the team that created the school's Mysteries Program. In the 1990s, I began to take these principles and practices into schools around the country, adapting, refining, and expanding the curriculum to include what I had learned from colleagues in the growing field of social and emotional learning. In those first years, I could not explain how Passages classes invited soul into the room. We do not use religious practices or even talking about religion. Yet the students reported that there was something "spiritual" about our classes. What did they mean?

Classrooms That Welcome Soul

- Why do I always act like everything is okay, when many times it's not?
- What am I supposed to learn from pain and suffering?
- How do I know how to do the right thing?
- Is this existence significant?
- Why did God make things so beautiful?
- Will people survive long enough to see the year 3000?
- When can I find out what to do to make relationships better?
- How do I integrate spirituality and human beingness in this life?

Most middle and high school students grapple with important questions about meaning, purpose, and ethical behavior. Of loss and love and letting go; of self-reliance and community; of choice and surrender. Even the youngest children startle us with their "big" questions. How they respond to these questions—whether with love, denial, or even violence—can be greatly influenced by the community of the classroom. When students work together to create an authentic community, they learn that they can meet any challenge with grace, with love, and with power—wrenching conflict, prejudice, profound gratitude, or even death. Creating authentic community is the first step toward this kind of learning.

When soul is present in education, attention shifts. We listen with great care not only to what is spoken but also to the messages between the words—tones, gestures, the flicker of feeling across the face. We concentrate on what has heart and meaning. The yearning, wonder, wisdom, fear, and confusion of students become central to the curriculum.

Questions become as important as answers.

When soul enters the classroom, masks drop away. Students venture to share the joy and talents they might have feared would provoke jealousy in even their best friends. They dare to risk exposing the pain or shame that might be judged as weakness. Seeing deeply into the perspectives of others, accepting what has felt unworthy in themselves, students discover compassion and begin to learn about forgiveness.

Inviting soul into education means giving students the skills to dive down into the deep well that is unique to each individual, and to meet at the underground stream that connects all the wells.[1] Inviting soul means acknowledging what is true—the good news and the bad. It means opening to what is ancient, wild, primeval.

How Can Teachers Invite Soul into the Classroom?

I will address this question on three levels: first, a framework for understanding what students, in their own words and experiences, find nourishing to their souls; second, a glance at methods and tools that can create the respect and openness in the classroom that allows young people to express what really matters to them; third, an exploration of how we as teachers can strengthen the personal qualities that allow students to trust us with their inner lives.

GATEWAYS TO THE SOUL

In my search to understand what could nourish the inner lives of students, rather than seek a framework from a religious or philosophical tradition I listened to the stories and questions of hundreds of students around the country. After many years, I began to see a pattern. It seemed that certain experiences quite apart from religious belief or affiliation had a powerful effect in nourishing the spiritual development of the young people I talked with. A map emerged—seven gateways to the soul of students—in which each gateway represents a set of key experiences embedded in their stories and questions.

- The search for meaning and purpose
- The longing for silence and solitude
- The urge for transcendence
- The hunger for joy and delight
- The creative drive
- The call for initiation
- The yearning for deep connection

Together, these gateways offer both a language and a framework for developing practical teaching strategies to invite soul into the classroom. Meeting these spiritual yearnings supports, strengthens, and fosters the development of a young person's spirit. Each of these gateways is explored in depth as a full chapter in my recent book *The Soul of Education: Helping Students Find Connection, Compassion and Character at School.* Here I will speak to the essence of each gateway for students.

1. *The search for meaning and purpose* concerns the exploration of existential questions that burst forth in adolescence. Why am I here? Does my life have a purpose? How do I find out what it is? What does my future hold? Is there life after death? Is there a God? These same questions arise time and again when students anonymously set down their "questions of wonder."

This domain of meaning and purpose is crucial to motivation and learning. It is also, paradoxically, both simple and uncomfortable for teachers to deal with. Teachers who predicate their authority on the ability to "know" or to have the "right answer" can be uncomfortable with questions that appear to have no agreed-upon answers. In most schools "purpose" is taught primarily through goal setting and decision making, often within strictly rational parameters. But if the inner life of adolescents is not cultivated as part of the search for goals or careers, they will most likely base their decisions on external pressures from peers, parents, teachers.

One student in my class wrote,

> So many of my friends are so clueless. They don't know what they want to do, they know what they're supposed to do. They don't know how they feel— they know how they're supposed to feel. And here I find myself in a group of people going through all my same stuff, and although I don't have the answers to all the questions, I find myself feeling like everything is perfect and right. . . . I have this "community" that gives me a home base and a sense of security.

Educators can provide experiences that honor the big questions. They can also allow students to give their gifts to the world through school and community service, through creative expression, or through academic or athletic achievement. In the way we teach, we can help students see and create patterns that connect learning to their personal lives. Another student described the impact of meaningful service on his life:

> When I go over to the local elementary school to tutor two Spanish-speaking children, they are so excited to see me. I guess they don't get too much attention from a teacher and a classroom that is strictly English speaking. . . . When I am with them, I feel special. I am an average student at my school, I don't hold any elected positions, I am not on any varsity team. I do not stand out in anyway, and that is okay with me. It is okay with me because for 3 hours each week, Maria and Miguel make me feel like I am the most important person in the world.

2. *The longing for silence and solitude* can lead to identity formation and goal setting, to learning readiness and inner peace. For adolescents, this domain is often ambivalent, fraught with both fear and urgent need. As a respite from the tyranny of busyness and noise that afflicts even our youngest children, silence may be a realm of reflection, calm, or fertile chaos—an avenue of stillness and rest for some, prayer or contemplation for others. "I like to take time to go within myself sometimes," another student wrote. "And when I do that, I try to take an emptiness inside there. I think that everyone struggles to find their own way with their spirit and it's in the struggle that our spirit comes forth.

3. *The urge for transcendence* describes the desire of young people to go beyond their perceived limits. "How far can I be stretched, how much adversity can I stand?" wrote one student. Another asked, "Is there a greater force at work? Can humans tap into that force, and bring it into their daily lives?" Transcendence includes not only the mystical realm, but also secular encounters with the extraordinary in the arts, athletics, academics, or human relations. By naming this human need that spans all cultures, educators can help students constructively channel this desire and challenge themselves to reach for transcendent experience in healthy ways.

4. *The hunger for joy and delight* can be satisfied through experiences of great simplicity, such as play, celebration, or gratitude. "I want to move many and take joy in every person, every little thing," wrote one student. Another asked, "Do all people have the same ca-

pacity to feel joy and sorrow?" Educators can also help students express the exaltation they feel when encountering beauty, power, grace, brilliance, love, or the sheer joy of being alive.

5. *The creative drive* is perhaps the most familiar domain for nourishing the spirit of students in secular schools. In opportunities for acts of creation—in the arts, problem solving, or originality in any field—students participate in a process infused with depth, meaning, and mystery. As one student put it, "There is something that happens to me in pottery class—I lose myself in the feeling of wet clay rolling smoothly under my hands as the wheel spins. I have it last period, so no matter how difficult the day was, pottery makes every day a good day. It's almost magical—to feel so good, so serene." And no one could express better the link between soul and creativity than an eighth grade girl who explained, "My creativity is the outreach of my spirit into form—so I can see it, hear it, feel it, touch it."

6. *The call for initiation* refers to a hunger many peoples have met through rites of passage. When we as elders do not take responsibility for consciously and constructively initiating our youth into adult society, young people often find ways that are destructive to claim their status as adults: hazing, drugs and alcohol, life-threatening risks, gangs, and premature sexuality become badges of adulthood. "If the fires that innately burn inside youths are not intentionally and lovingly added to the hearth of community," says poet Michael Meade, "they will burn down the structures of culture, just to feel the warmth."[2]

As educators, we can create programs that guide adolescents through the irrevocable transition from childhood to adulthood by giving them tools for making transitions and separations, challenging them to discover their own capacities, and creating ceremonies that acknowledge and welcome them into the community of adults.

7. *The common thread is deep connection.* As my students tell stories about each of these domains, I hear a common thread: the experience of deep connection, a quality of relationship that is profoundly caring and resonant with meaning, feelings of belonging, and a sense of being truly seen or known.

Through *deep connection to the self,* students encounter a strength and richness within that is the basis for developing the autonomy central to the adolescent journey, to discovering purpose and unlocking creativity. Teachers can nourish this form of deep connection by giving students time for solitary reflection. Classroom exercises that encourage expression through writing or art can also allow a student access to his or her inner self even while in the midst of other people. Totally engrossed in creative activities, students are encouraged to discover and express their own feelings, values, and beliefs.

By *connecting deeply to another person or group,* young people discover the balm of belonging, which soothes the profound alienation that can fracture their identity and prevent them from contributing to our communities. To feel a sense of belonging at school, students must be part of an authentic community in the classroom—a community in which they feel seen and heard for who they really are. Many teachers create this opportunity through morning meetings, weekly councils, or "sharing circles" offered in the context of ground rules that make it safe to be vulnerable. The challenge for the teacher is to support the autonomy and uniqueness of each individual while fostering a sense of belonging and union within the group. The more young people are encouraged to strengthen their own boundaries and develop their own identities, the more capable they will be of bonding to a group in a healthy, enduring way.

Some students *connect deeply to nature.* "When I get depressed," revealed Keisha to her "family group" members in a school in Manhattan, "I go to this park near my house where there is an absolutely enormous tree. I go and sit down with it because it feels so strong to me." "It was my science teacher who awakened my spirit," said one teacher about his high school days in Massachusetts. "He conveyed a sense of awe about the natural world that would change me forever."

And some students discover solace in *their relationship to a faith tradition.* "I try to practice being present," one student wrote. "That's what Buddhism has given to me that I really cherish. It's really the most important thing to me now." Another said, "I became a Christian a few years back. It's been the most wonderful thing in my life. I can't tell you what it feels like to know that I'm loved like that. Always loved and guided. By Jesus. And it's brought our family much closer."

When students know that there is a place in school life for giving voice to the great comfort and joy they find in their relationship to their God or to nature, this freedom of expression nourishes their spirits. In fact, the First Amendment protects students' freedom of expression, including the expression of religious faith. We teachers must be careful not to share our own religious or antireligious beliefs, since given the power and public nature of our role, students may experience this as proselytizing; but the First Amendment principle of the separation of church and state does not require us to suppress the rich exchange that comes when such an important part of students' lives is acknowledged and respected.

Young people who feel deeply connected don't need danger to feel fully alive. They don't need guns to feel powerful. They don't want to hurt others or themselves. Out of connection grows compassion and passion—passion for people, for our goals and dreams, for life itself.

A GLANCE AT METHODOLOGY

To achieve the safety and openness required for meaningful exploration of spiritual development, students and teachers must work together carefully for weeks and months. It is helpful to collaboratively create *agreements*—conditions that students name as essential for speaking about what matters most to them.

Play helps students focus, relax, and become part of a team through laughter and cooperation. *Symbols and metaphors* that students create or bring into class allow them to speak indirectly about feelings and thoughts that are awkward to address head-on; they provide a language that takes students easily to depths that are otherwise hard to access. *The arts* offer students a variety of modalities to express themselves in ways that match or stretch their natural learning styles.

Honoring questions opens the door for a deeper understanding of what is rumbling in the hearts of young people. Once a climate of respect and trustworthiness is well established, students are invited to anonymously submit the questions that capture their wonder, worry, curiosity, fear, excitement, and confusion. Hundreds of questions like those above and below emerge from each classroom community.

- Why am I here? Does my life have a purpose? How do I find it?
- Why this emptiness in this world, in my heart?
- Why does violence have to be the answer to everything?

- Is there anyone out in the world like me?
- Why do people hate others—black, white, Hispanic, etc.?
- Why do people do drugs?
- Why do people talk before thinking?
- Why are people so careless with our planet?

Such questions help students discover that they are not alone and guide teachers in refining the curriculum for the particular needs of each group.

We use the *council process,* a highly structured form of conversation that allows each person to speak without interruption or immediate response.[3] Sitting in a circle, where everyone can be seen, students speak about themes set by the teacher in response to their own questions, to issues raised by academic content, or to developmental concerns. An atmosphere of heightened respect is created with the use of simple rituals designed to honor—never to violate—the diversity of family beliefs and traditions. Students learn to listen deeply and discover what it feels like to be truly heard. *Silence* becomes a comfortable ally as we pause to digest one story and wait for another to form, or when teachers call for moments of reflection, or when the room fills with feeling at the end of a class.

Welcoming the inner life to school in these ways takes many forms.

An English teacher in an inner-city high school in Washington, D.C., provides art materials for students to symbolically express their feelings, goals, and strengths. As they discuss the assigned literature, they shift periodically into telling stories from their own lives that relate to the struggles of the characters in their books.

A health educator in Colorado provides a "transitions" course for ninth graders, weaving social and emotional skills and opportunities for expression together with study skills and health issues. "Mysteries questions" are shared, with students' permission, with the academic faculty, who are often awed and amazed by both the hidden wisdom and the pain expressed by students they see every day. After a year of resisting the idea of initiating a comprehensive program to address heart, soul, and community, this faculty begins to voice enthusiasm and curiosity about next steps.

An eighth grade English teacher organizes the entire year's curriculum around the themes of relationship and love, selecting literature that relates to these concerns. In addition to reading, analytical discussion, and writing, her students keep personal journals to express their own feelings about these themes. Once a week they sit in council, relating stories and feelings from their own lives that have been stirred by the required readings. At the end of the year, she designs activities for a field trip that will provide a simple but meaningful rite of passage from middle school to high school.

A second grade teacher in New York integrates a sharing circle weekly into her contained classroom, using games, art, and movement to awaken the realm of imagination and soul and to help the children make the transition from academic learning to the more vulnerable territory of personal expression.

A "TEACHING PRESENCE"

We have taken a look at the kinds of experiences that young people report are most supportive of their inner lives, and considered methods that contribute to creating a classroom that welcomes such experiences. But beyond technique, conceptual understanding, and curriculum, the most effective teaching also includes the quality of our own presence—what is commonly known in our profession as modeling.

"We teach who we are." "Walk your talk." Or, as Ralph Waldo Emerson put it, "What you are speaks so loudly that I can't hear what you say you are."

Our way of being in the world of the classroom—whether we are "being peace" or "being impatience," "being respect" or "being condescension," "being awareness" or "being numb"—will ultimately determine how safe and open students will feel when we invite them to explore deep matters.[4] Students are very sensitive to the qualities of their guides. We can have the best curricula available, train teachers in technique and theory, but our students will be unsafe and our programs hollow if we do not provide opportunities for teachers to develop their own souls, their own social and emotional intelligence. Students are reluctant to open their hearts unless they feel that their teachers are on the same journey themselves—working on personal as well as curriculum integration.

We are more likely to create authentic forums for our students if we have explored our own relationship to the gateways that nourish the soul of students. I offer here a series of questions and exercises that may support this process. These suggestions may provide a springboard for a teacher or counselor to create his or her own approach for meeting students in their search for meaning, silence, joy, creativity, transcendence, initiation, and deep connection.

But there is something more—something elusive—that determines the quality of our teaching. We celebrate those precious moments when we embody a presence that carries the class to a place where minds and hearts are moved and genuine connections occur. Some teachers just naturally live there most of the time. But how do we find that place? What are the unspoken messages we transmit through our very being that determine whether students feel safe and welcome in the classroom? How can we embody the qualities that will invite them to share experiences of what has touched them deeply, what is important in their lives, what they yearn for or feel confused or concerned about?

I have wrestled with this question over the last fifteen years as I have worked with thousands of adolescents, teachers, and counselors. As I witnessed myself and others feel "on" one day and "off" the next, I felt called to find words to describe this elusive state I call "the teaching presence" and to help teachers strengthen this aspect of their work.

Let us look now at three qualities—discipline, presence, and an open heart—that define the "teaching presence" in the classroom.

RESPECTFUL DISCIPLINE

> To believe that one can teach respect through
> coercion is to confuse respect with obedience.
> —Larry Brendtro and Nicholas Long, *Reclaiming
> Children and Youth.*

If we want our classrooms to be places for students to share what is deeply meaningful to them, we must take responsibility for creating an environment that is safe. Only then will they respond with their hearts and spirits and risk asking fundamental questions. A teacher cannot create safe space alone—this is a goal and a process that must be shared by the whole group. But the teacher is the guide for how a safe place is created for the human heart and the shepherd who protects when danger appears. Respectful discipline is an essential tool in creating this safety.

A respectful climate encourages children to speak from the heart. Speaking from the heart is what makes a class come alive; it is what engages other children to want to listen. And when they listen to someone speaking from this depth and vulnerability, their own hearts open to that person and they feel compassion. What was at first good classroom behavior becomes true respect for someone they may have previously disliked or dismissed.

Each teacher must find his or her own words to convey simply and clearly the purpose of welcoming a more personal dimension to learning. Then he or she can create a partnership with students to establish the conditions for safety that will allow authentic dialogue to unfold. Early in the semester, I ask students, "What are the conditions or agreements you need so you can be fully yourself here—so you can take risks to grow and learn, so you can talk about what matters deeply to you?" I write down their words and encourage them to clarify their needs:

- listening for understanding
- no put-downs, "bagging," or "dissing"
- openness
- respect
- honesty
- the right to be silent
- honor given to the privacy of what is spoken

Together we make a list, which looks remarkably similar from class to class, region to region, and year to year.

When ground rules are created collaboratively, students take ownership of these boundaries and are far more likely to honor them. Yet ultimately it is the teacher's responsibility to ensure that students and the learning process are protected. Many teachers have a negative image of discipline, confusing firmness with authoritarian repression. My own views of discipline began to change in the late 1970s, in response to the wisdom of a colleague with forty years of experience with children. "Children do not always know yet what is safe for them or others," said Dorothy. "Discipline and limits are a way that we create a circle of safety for those not yet ready to do this for themselves. Picture these limits as a big hug—our strong arms encircling the child with comfort and safety."

Once we see discipline as an act of love and containment, we can be creative and responsive to the style and degree of discipline needed with a particular child or group. I encourage teachers to seek their own metaphors to help them discover a positive outlook on discipline. When we distinguish respect from fear and provide limits to prevent children from harming each other, we are not defending our power as teachers; we are helping group members create the safety to be vulnerable and authentic with one another.

Finally, we can become conscious of and learn to use the full range of our personal power to command respect. Gesture, humor, voice, eyes, and emotional expression—our whole selves—can convey respectful discipline.

Knowing that their vulnerability will be respected and protected, both teachers and students can begin to open their hearts, to connect deeply with themselves and one another, and risk bringing their full humanity to the classroom.

AN OPEN HEART

An open heart is a precondition to being fully present. A teacher with an open heart can be warm, alive, spontaneous, connected, compassionate. He or she can see the language of the body and hear the feelings between the words. An open heart is what allows a teacher to be trustworthy and to help build trust among his or her students.

To have an open heart, a teacher must be willing to be vulnerable and willing to care.

Vulnerability. To be vulnerable is to be willing to feel deeply, to be moved by what a student expresses or by what comes up inside ourselves in the presence of our students or the issues they raise. According to the dictionary, "vulnerable" means "susceptible to injury, insufficiently defended." It comes from the Latin for "to wound." It implies danger and risk. This potential for being wounded is a clue to the challenge of teaching with an open heart.

Leading our students to express their emotions and respond fully to others, we are more effective and trustworthy if we are a part of the group ourselves, rather than placing ourselves apart from or above that circle of genuine feeling. But vulnerability is not to be confused with a failure to set boundaries. Indeed, it is not until a teacher has developed such boundaries that he or she can afford to be truly open with students without losing his or her own center.

Even teachers who have learned to be vulnerable with young people may go through periods when it is difficult to do so. When we are emotionally raw, we need our walls to protect us and to protect others from our volatile impulses. Since we all have such times, how do we keep our hearts open in the face of stress or grief?

First, we acknowledge it to ourselves. Just allowing ourselves to become conscious about our defenses helps keep the heart open to others. Reflection and contemplation can help us scan our hearts and acknowledge difficult feelings to ourselves.

Second, we can acknowledge our pain to people who can help us cope, understand, and heal. It is precisely at these times that we don't share feelings with students, so a teacher must have resources— friends, colleagues, a therapist or supervisor—and must be willing to use these resources. Creating regular opportunities when teachers can support each other personally has been an important feature of my work in social and emotional learning. Group supervision meetings can provide a safe container for teachers' feelings. Support for maintaining an open heart is particularly important because exposing ourselves to the volatile emotions of children or adolescents can stir some of our own deepest issues.

Willingness to care. What does it mean for a teacher to be willing to care deeply about his or her students? I believe that teachers cannot really develop the "teaching presence" without being willing and able to love. Knowing the limitations of children's developing capacities for perspective, social skill, or self-mastery, a loving teacher feels deep respect for the essential humanity—the depth of feeling and capacity for wisdom—in even the smallest child.

I once had a conversation with an elderly relative who declared that some people are interesting and others have nothing to say. I tried to speak respectfully when I responded that in my work I had found that any person who feels safe enough to speak from the heart is interesting to listen to. I have often been surprised anew when an apparently superficial, rebellious, or dull young person is moved by love and respect to speak with a tenderness, depth, and wisdom.

A teacher's love is at the heart of effective discipline. Love does not tolerate behavior that is abusive to anyone. But love does accept and forgive the child from whom this behavior springs.

Obstacles to caring. The first obstacle to caring is the fear of loss or rejection. We may feel that if we care deeply, we give a person more power to hurt us. How much safer it seems to mute our willingness to care.

"Doing it right" can also be an obstacle to caring. When we are totally focused on "covering the material," preoccupied with competence and success, we often forget to open our hearts to our students. Particularly if they are "sabotaging" the "success" of the group, we may shut down. Coaching one new teacher, I simply had to say kindly that she appeared to be so concerned about doing a good job that she had forgotten to engage with her students. Her instant recognition that this was so transformed her teaching.

Our hearts can also become blocked when we are attached to a particular plan, technique, or approach in the classroom. If we can keep our hearts open, we can see the unique needs of our students and discover entirely different ways to reach our larger goals. This capacity to care deeply about our students and about our mission without being attached to a specific, "known" outcome on a given day is crucial to the art of being fully present in the classroom.

Such caring and responsiveness need not conflict with high academic goals. In fact, it is often the precondition for improved achievement. After years of struggle and failure, a student whose academic performance had dramatically improved explained to alternative high school teacher John McCluskey, "Because you held our hearts last year, I discovered that my brain could work."

BEING PRESENT

"The present moment is one of power, of magic or miracle if we could ever be wholly in it and awake to it," writes D. M. Dooling.[5] Chogyam Trungpa puts it this way: "The way to experience nowness is to realize that this very moment, this very point in your life, is always the occasion."[6]

Being fully present is the very heart of "the teaching presence." A teacher is expressing this capacity when he or she is

- open to perceiving what is happening right now,
- responsive to the needs of this moment,
- flexible enough to shift gears,
- prepared with the repertoire, creativity, and imagination to invent a new approach in the moment,
- humble and honest enough to simply pause and acknowledge if a new approach has not yet arrived.

Being present can mean letting go of a particular approach. It may also mean letting go of the goal of that day's class. Is this goal more important than what is coming up in the moment? We must wrestle with this question because the answer is always different. If we have developed our capacities for discipline, we will not change course just because students complain or get sidetracked. But sometimes our larger vision of the purpose of this class, which transcends the goal of a particular lesson plan, reveals an opportunity for students to learn better now what we might have planned to cover two months from now. Being present allows us to recognize these "teachable moments" and take advantage of them to enhance learning and see the bigger picture.

Being present also means the ability to see that when things are going "wrong"—the air conditioning keeps breaking, or the group is always tired because this class is scheduled for the last period on Friday—there may be an opportunity for students to learn something about meeting a challenge.

How can we be present if we come into class with a load of baggage, preoccupied or exhausted by the events of our lives? Most of the things that trouble us—a fight with a colleague, a personal family matter, a disturbing dream—are too private, as we've said, to be shared appropriately with our students. Particularly at a time when so many children are being enrolled to parent their own parents, children need adult role models who can authentically and gracefully care for their own needs without imposing them on children.

What are the ways that teachers can express and contain their own feelings before coming into class? What supports can we provide teachers so they can be resilient and remain responsive and creative with their students?

Cultivating presence has both psychological and spiritual dimensions. Teachers, like other people, need sources of psychological support for processing emotions and issues in order to be more in charge of and more at peace with themselves. As I discussed in the section on keeping our hearts open, schools or departments that are committed to welcoming the inner life can best sustain teachers by building in such emotional support through supervision or faculty meetings that include personal councils. On a day-to-day level, teachers caught off guard by a sudden upset can seek a friend or colleague with whom to share feelings so they don't spill over into class.

The spiritual dimension is more elusive. "We tend to postpone being alive to the future," writes Thich Nhat Hanh, poet, Zen master, and peace activist, in his book *Being Peace,* and our orientation toward the future keeps many of us from experiencing the fullness of the present, the fullness of life. Dwelling on the past—either idealizing it or obsessing about our wounds—is also an obstacle to being present. Much within our traditional educational models and ways of raising children is based on a veneration of the past. We must find ways to use the gifts of the past while remaining fully present.

Becoming fully present is a priority for both student and teacher in my approach to teaching. I believe it is my responsibility as a teacher to help students come into the here and now so that we can all learn together. Games wake them up; quiet reflection invites them to look inside and release distracting thoughts and feelings. Pairing or group sharing exercises allow students to express what may be preoccupying them and so to let it go. When we have created a safe enough classroom for students to "speak from the heart," such authentic expression is riveting, calling both speaker and listener into the present moment.

Many teachers have shared with me their own approaches to cultivating this being in the present: running, hiking, playing a musical instrument, painting, meditation, writing poetry, or keeping a daily journal are all processes that allow one to clear the mind of distractions. Most agree that discovering this quality of being is a spiritual experience. In those rare times when I have spent an entire day or several days in a state of being present, I have felt my strongest connection to my spirit and to the exquisite gift of life.

It takes courage for teachers to work with students at the level of heart and soul. Entering this arena—particularly with adolescents— can drop us into the cauldron of our own emotional and spiritual growth. But the rewards are great for teachers who are willing to engage their own depths, meeting the demons and the allies that dwell within.

Questions and Exercises for Teachers

The following questions and exercises are one way of exploring your relationship to the "seven gateways." Because they are designed to take you to the depths of yourself, I encourage you to approach them carefully. If you choose to do the exercises with a colleague or group of colleagues, be sure to spend time first creating a set of ground rules that you all feel will enable vulnerability to be safe and appropriate.

MEANING AND PURPOSE

Questions:

- What do I know about my purpose or mission in life? What have been the clues?
- Looking back at my life, is there a thread of connection through apparently disparate choices and events?
- When unexpectedly challenged by suffering or adversity, how do I respond?

Exercises:

- Write your own "questions of wonder." What do you wonder about? Worry about? Feel afraid of? Curious about? Excited about? What do you think about when you can't sleep at night?

- Reflect on how your questions compare to those from your students.

SILENCE AND SOLITUDE

Questions:

- How do I feel about silence when I am alone? When I am with one other person? In the midst of a classroom discussion? In the midst of a faculty meeting?
- Has my experience of silence or solitude changed in my life? How? When?
- When was the last time I spent a day alone? How do I feel when I answer this question?

Exercises:

- For the next month, create a consistent time each day for ten minutes of silence and solitude. Experiment with different ways to use this time: walking, sitting, writing or drawing about what you are feeling, lying down (but not dozing).
- Choose one hour to be silent and alone during which you experiment with aimlessness: do not write or draw or read or sleep or jog. You can sit still or choose to walk aimlessly.

TRANSCENDENCE

Questions:

- Have I ever surprised myself by surpassing a limit I thought was fixed and firm inside of me? In what domain of life? Academics? Athletics? Relationship? Prejudice? Suffering? Joy? Other?
- Have I had what I would describe as a "peak" moment or experience in my life?
- What are my beliefs and feelings about my experiences with mental states outside of ordinary thought?

Exercises:

- Write about a moment or experience in your life that felt "special" in some way—a time that felt like it was outside of your ordinary way of living or feeling.

- Create an opportunity to talk with colleagues about "peak" experiences. Explore why it is difficult to share these experiences. How do you feel if you have never had an experience you would describe in this way?

JOY

Questions:

- How do I feel about play? About dance? Singing? Which of these activities are fun for me? Uncomfortable?
- How do I feel when other people are joyful and I am not? When I am joyful and others are not?
- For what am I grateful right now in my life?
- Which of my senses give me the greatest pleasure? What was I taught to believe about sensual pleasure? What do I believe now?

Exercises:

- Write about the history of joy in your life, exploring some of the questions above. Capture the places, kinds of people, and activities in which you tend to feel the most delight.
- Identify an obstacle within you to experiencing joy and write about that obstacle. When did it first appear? When does it surface now? Carry on a dialogue with it.

CREATIVITY

Questions:

- In what arena of my life do I feel creative?
- What supports my creative expression and what gets in the way?
- Is there a form of creativity I envy in others?

Exercises:

- Make a date with yourself to express your creativity. Choose a form you have been longing to try. Write some reflections on the experience.

- Create a faculty meeting in which each person has the opportunity, if they want to, to share some aspect of their creative expression: a work of art or craft, a challenging problem they have solved, a new approach to teaching they have invented, etc.

INITIATION

Questions:

- How do I handle transitions in my own life?
- How do I relate to other people in transition?
- Which transitions were difficult for me? Puberty? The shift from middle to high school? The end of high school? The beginning or end of college?
- Were there any adults in my life who served as mentors, guides, or allies during these transitions?

Exercises:

- Write about your most recent significant life transition. What supported you from the inside and outside in navigating this transition safely? What made it difficult?
- Write a letter to someone who has served in your life as an elder. Tell them how they have supported you. Send the letter or file it in your journal. If you cannot think of a single elder, write a letter to someone who you wished had been your elder and tell them how you feel.

DEEP CONNECTION

Questions about inner connectedness:

- What allows you to be deeply connected to yourself? What prevents you from being deeply connected to yourself? How has this changed over time?
- What supports you in overcoming these obstacles?

Exercise:

- Make a list of what allows you to be deeply connected to yourself. Share your list with a friend or colleague. Commit to making room for one of these experiences in each day for a week. Ask your partner to hold you accountable—report back at the end of the week to this partner about how this experiment went for you.

Questions about connection to others:

- How do you define intimacy?
- What allows you to connect deeply to another person? In yourself? In the other?
- What can make it hard for you to get close to others?

Exercises:

- With a partner, or with a small group (where you have created ground rules for safety), share stories about a time when someone you trusted let you down or when you let someone down, or a time when a person surprised you by coming through for you when you least expected it or when you surprised someone else with your trustworthiness.
- Write about an experience of feeling deeply connected to another. How did this closeness evolve? Was the closeness ever challenged? Did you overcome that challenge—if so, how? What is the place of that person in your life today? How do you feel about this relationship?

Questions about connection to community:

- What kind of groups feel comfortable for you? Uncomfortable?
- Do you take a certain role in groups? Leader, observer, clown, rebel?
- Have you been part of a group that felt like a real community to you? What does "real community" mean to you?

Exercise:

- Experiment in your next faculty meeting or family gathering with playing a different role than the one you are used to. Observe how you feel. Observe how others respond to you.

Questions about connection to nature, to lineage, to a higher power:

- Do you feel a deep connection to any of these larger sources of meaning? Which ones? If not, how does that feel for you? If so, what experiences have encouraged the development of this connection?

Exercises:

- Draw or write a list of stepping-stones over your lifetime in your relationship to a larger source of meaning. Note times of particular connection or disconnection or cynicism.
- Take one or two of these stepping-stones and draw them out further. Explore what else was going on at that time in terms of your relationships, your body, your place of home and work or school, the moment in the history of your place or the globe.

Nourishing the hearts of students, our own souls are fed. We find a renewal of our passion for teaching and a long-term recipe for avoiding burnout. If we bring to the classroom an open mind, a heart full of love, and a will strong enough to protect and guide, we can cultivate there the kind of atmosphere that invites students to safely explore the social, emotional, and spiritual realms of life. In both their professional and personal lives, teachers who do so will discover the rewards of tremendous insight and personal strength.

PARKER J. PALMER, WITH MARCY JACKSON,
RICK JACKSON, AND DAVID SLUYTER

The Courage to Teach:
A Program for Teacher Renewal

*T*hrough these retreats, I have rediscovered a generosity of heart
and developed a taste for suffering."

The teacher who spoke those words after participating in a two-
year series of "Courage to Teach" retreats is a better teacher today than
before his transformation, and better able to endure the demands of a
teacher's life. But in what voice is he speaking? It is not the voice of the
ego, which normally speaks in tones of pride or fear. Nor is it the professional voice, which normally speaks about "content areas" and
"methodology." It is, instead, the voice of the soul, that sacred place in
every human being where suffering is transformed into creativity and
from which generosity can flow.

The Courage to Teach program, which began in 1994 and is now
at work in cities across the country, builds on a simple premise:
teachers who are disconnected from their souls cannot serve their
students well, let alone invite the student's soul into the educational
process. Good teachers possess much more than information and
technique. They possess "a capacity for connectedness." They offer

up soul, or selfhood, as the loom on which to weave a fabric of connectedness between themselves, their students, their subjects, and the world.

On Soul, Role, and Formation

Helping teachers connect soul and role through a process called formation is what the Courage to Teach program is designed to do. Sadly, our professional training, with its mythology of objectivism, treats soul and selfhood not as assets but as liabilities, dangerous sources of subjectivity that would taint the work professionals do. So the bad news is that formation happens in an ethos that is often hostile to the very premises on which formation stands. But the good news is that more and more teachers are seeking ways to do authentic inner work for the sake of their professional growth, precisely because they have been so constrained, even wounded, by that objectivist ethos.

We chose the word "formation" to name this inner work because it is an ancient term used by many spiritual traditions to describe "the cure of the soul." We believe that everyone comes into the world with a perfectly formed soul. But, as time goes on, the soul is increasingly deformed by forces both external and internal: externally by forces like racism and sexism, internally by forces like ego-anxiety and ego-inflation.

In the context of our work as educators, "formation" involves the creation of open, resourceful, and trustworthy spaces where teachers, in solitude and community, can allow the soul to escape those forces of deformation and reclaim its original form. The soul alone knows what its true form is. Our task is to create situations safe enough for the soul to speak its own truth—and quiet enough for the person to hear what it has to say.

We are guided in this work by a clear image of the nature of the human soul. The soul is like a wild animal: it is tough, resilient, savvy, and self-sufficient, and yet it is exceedingly shy. If we want to see a wild animal, the last thing we should do is go crashing through the woods shouting for the creature to come out. But if we are willing to walk quietly into the woods and sit silently for an hour or two at the base of

a tree, the creature we are waiting for may well emerge; out of the corner of an eye we will catch a glimpse of the precious wildness we
seek—and we will never forget the sight.

This image has practical implications for what goes on in a formation retreat. From the outset, we tell retreatants that this is not a "share
or die" event. If the facilitator invites participants to form small
groups but what you need at the moment is solitude, or a stroll, or a
nap, you are encouraged to do what you need—with the full support
of the community. Your soul knows its needs far better than anyone
else does.

When we go into small groups with the invitation to share an issue
or a problem, a few simple and straightforward ground rules allow us
to sit quietly in the woods with each other: no advising, no fixing, no
saving, no setting straight. That is, no invading. Instead, we are to listen to each other at a depth that will "hear each other into speech"—a
listening that is enhanced by asking honest, open questions that might
evoke more of what the speaker is trying to say. What the soul wants is
not to be fixed or saved but simply to be received and heard.

Trustworthy space requires boundaries to help guide the formation process toward matters of meaning; without boundaries, space
becomes a frightening void. So one of our challenges in developing
the Courage to Teach program was to find a way of framing the formation space that would draw teachers into exploring the deepest
spiritual issues of their lives but would do so without giving offense or
creating barriers in a society that is both secular and religiously pluralistic.

To achieve this balance, we turned to the metaphors offered by the
cycle of the seasons, which provide powerful ways of evoking the
questions closest to the soul so that our inquiry is bounded without
leaving anyone feeling trapped in a doctrinal or dogmatic box.

The Courage to Teach program begins in the fall, the season when
nature is scattering seeds for the growth that is yet to come. In this season we ask people to reflect on "the seed of true self" that was planted
when they were born, by telling stories from their childhood or about
their first moments of an awareness that they felt called to teach.
Through those stories they start to reclaim the birthright gifts and
passions that put them on this vocational path.

In the winter season we raise questions about darkness and death, dormancy and renewal. Some of the seeds we brought into the world, or planted once we got here, are now underground, and may indeed have died. But others rest in a time of dormancy, awaiting another season, a season of rebirth. Only when we can see the potentials that lie dormant in ourselves can we see the same in another—and what are our students but bundles of dormancies?

Spring is the season of rebirth, so in the spring we reflect on "the flowering of paradox." It is a great paradox that what once seemed dead is now alive, and not only alive but beautiful! Authentic education is full of such paradoxes, if we have eyes to see, for it involves the death of old ideas and assumptions and the emergence of new forms of knowing and being in the world.

Summer is the season of abundance and harvest. In this season we pursue questions about generosity and the gifts we possess within us that we may not even be aware of. We ask how that abundance may be intended to feed others, whether they be students or colleagues or the larger community.

In the Courage to Teach program we pursue this seasonal cycle, or let it pursue us, through eight retreats over a span of two years. Not only does this allow for the slow growth of the soul and of authentic community—for slowly is the only way such things grow—but it also allows us to do what we must do in the spiritual life: return to the same season again and again and again.

The work of formation is more akin to farming or gardening than it is to manufacturing. The manufacturer starts with "raw material" and adds value to it through a controlled and predictable process. But the farmer, who works not with raw material but with living organisms, must start all over each year through an eternal return of the seasons, and must embrace the fact that not everything that happens in one particular cycle is under his or her control: the rains may not come, the hail may wipe out the crops.

Whether our concern is with teachers or students or both, the agricultural model is far more faithful to the way people learn than is the manufacturing model that has dominated the conduct of much of American education. Using seasonal metaphors rids us of the hubris of believing that we can control human growth. They help us understand how interdependent we are with all the life forms around us—an understanding that can help us grow into teachers who know how to cultivate the young.

How Formation Happens

The Courage to Teach program was piloted in southwest Michigan from 1994 to 1996, under the direction of Parker J. Palmer and with the support of the Fetzer Institute, a Michigan-based philanthropic foundation. The overwhelmingly positive response to the pilot led Fetzer to test the model via four new programs (1996 to 1998) in South Carolina, Maryland–District of Columbia, Michigan, and Washington State.

In 1998, the Center for Teacher Formation was established on Bainbridge Island, near Seattle, and through its offices new Courage to Teach programs have been developed, or are under development, in Massachusetts, Michigan, Minnesota, Maryland, Oregon, North Carolina, New Mexico, South Carolina, Texas, Vermont, Wisconsin, and Washington State.

Courage to Teach is focused on K-12 educators in the public schools—the teachers, administrators, and counselors upon whom our society depends for so much but for whom we provide so little encouragement and support. Each retreat group consists of twenty to thirty participants, selected from a pool of applicants, who stay together through eight quarterly retreats of three days or four days each over a two-year period under the guidance of a facilitator trained and accredited by the Center for Teacher Formation.

In applying for the program, teachers and administrators consistently attest to their deep need for the kind of renewal the Courage to Teach hopes to offer:

> I don't need another in-service, nor do I need more opportunities to work on systemic reform. I'm already deeply involved in that! I need the chance to concentrate on my emotional and spiritual growth so that I am able to once again teach truly from the heart.

> There are times when I'm not sure I can make it, when the pain of so many of the young lives I get wrapped up in threatens to swamp my own life and I fear I will be of no use to anyone. I also know that I reach children and that what I do is of value. . . . When this pamphlet arrived, I was astonished. A renewal program for teachers? Inner life? Mine is far beneath my bed, gathering dust.

Friends urge me to move to an "easier" school, but I want to find a way to cope with the stress and enable myself to continue reaching out to these kids. I know that there are people out there who can do this and thrive. I want to be one of them.

I want to be able to accept the realities of education without having to become disillusioned, bored and disgruntled. I am a young teacher. Twenty years from now, I still want to say with passion that I am doing exactly what I want to do.

In response to needs such as these, the retreats run by Courage to Teach focus neither on "technique" nor on school reform, but on renewing the inner lives of public school educators. In large-group, small-group, and solitary settings, we use a variety of approaches to engage teachers and administrators in discovering or recovering their "inner teacher."

To give the reader a concrete sense of what a Courage to Teach retreat involves—and how it may differ from other approaches to professional and personal development—we want to describe six fundamentals involved in structuring and guiding these retreats:

1. Framing evocative questions
2. Welcoming silence
3. Working with paradox
4. Identifying birthright gifts
5. Using poetry and teaching stories as "third things"
6. Practicing the "clearness committee"

1. *Framing evocative questions:* At the outset of a retreat, and at various points in midstream, we raise reflective questions as a way of checking in with each other. These questions are designed both to evoke meaningful reflection and to connect us with the larger context of our work, and they often come in pairs to invite teachers to reflect on the complex relationship between vocation and selfhood.

For example, the question, What aspects of your identity and integrity feel most supported or engaged by the work you do? is asked hand in hand with, What aspects of your identity and integrity feel most threatened or endangered by the work you do? This paradoxical pair requires a more complex awareness of oneself and one's work situation than do the questions, What do you like best about your work? and, What do you like least about your work?

Before retreatants answer a question in the large group, we invite them to take some time for reflection, and perhaps some journaling. Then, rather than marching around the circle with each person sharing in turn, we invite people to speak if and as they feel ready, and we encourage silence in the spaces between individual reflections.

2. *Welcoming silence:* Words are not the only medium of exchange and learning in the work of formation. We share and grow in silence as well, not only because silence gives us a chance to reflect upon and absorb what we have said and heard, but because a silence is itself a sort of speech from the deepest parts of ourselves, of others, of the world. The typical group, psychologists tell us, can abide about fifteen seconds of silence before someone will feel the need to speak in order to "break the tension." In the Courage to Teach program we work hard to make sure that both silence and speech become trustworthy shared practices for our explorations of the soul.

Though it is startling at first to teachers who are accustomed to being task-oriented and making "maximal use of minimal time," we often begin our group sessions with extended silences, and we invite silences in the midst of our conversations and activities, including the practice of silent breaks. This helps create a slower, more reflective pace for discussion and enables participants to listen to the inner teacher as closely as they listen to the insights of others.

3. *Working with paradox:* Like the field that a farmer prepares in order to grow a crop, a formation space must possess several qualities in order to allow the seed of true self to germinate. These qualities, like so much in the inner world, may seem on the surface to be contradictory but in truth complement and co-create each other.

This kind of paradox is at the very heart of the inner life: you cannot know light without darkness, silence without speech, solitude without community. And between the poles of paradox runs a continuum along which almost anyone can find his or her current condition, and thus a level of comfort with what we are doing.

In creating a formation space, we are guided by six key paradoxes (see Chapter 3 of Parker J. Palmer's *The Courage to Teach*), one of which is that a good formation space must be simultaneously "hospitable" and "charged."

A hospitable space is one that people find not only free but warmly inviting, not only open but safe and trustworthy, a reliably nonjudgmental space in which people can find the security they need to sustain dangerous journeys. At the same time, the space must be "charged" if the journey is to be real and rewarding. There must be a sense of electricity, of risk, of stakes, of the danger inherent in pursuing the deep things of the human soul. We do not need to create this charge as a "special effect"—it comes with the territory. We only need to bound or define the space with topics of significance and refuse to trivialize those topics in any way.

4. *Identifying birthright gifts:* Many of us have no trouble listing our weaknesses or failures, but we find it difficult to acknowledge our strengths and gifts. It is as if we have blinders on that keep us from seeing ourselves whole. In formation it becomes crucial to uncover, or recover, those gifts, strengths, and sensibilities with which each of us is endowed.

These "birthright gifts" are not the skills we went to college or graduate school to develop, nor are they the areas in which we have worked hard to excel. Rather, they are the qualities that are part of our very nature, qualities that have been apparent to others since we were young children, but which we ourselves may have devalued, ignored, or simply failed to recognize.

When we honor a person's gifts, we honor that person's soul. Given the beleaguered state of most teachers, and the recent wave of teacher-bashing in the media and other public forums, naming and claiming birthright gifts is often experienced by participants as one of the most rewarding early features of our program's retreats.

But the importance of this exercise goes beyond the enhancement of self-esteem. When we are in touch with our own giftedness we are much more likely to notice and draw out the gifts of others—our peers and colleagues as well as the children we teach—and education itself is enhanced. When colleagues respect each other's gifts, the community of teaching is strengthened. And when teachers respect their students' gifts, the community of learning expands.

5. Using poetry and teaching stories as "third things": In the work called formation, it is vital to understand that truth is not a single point or even a linear argument made up of many points. Instead, truth is a tapestry or a collage, a rich pattern of meaning that is generated by the whole group, a pattern in which every member of the group can find himself or herself. So in retreats that try to reach deep into the truth of our teaching lives, we use stories and poems from diverse sources, for stories and poems are the ways in which human beings have always expressed this more complex form of truth.

Using stories and poems as "third things" to mediate between facilitator and participants puts a plumb line down the center of the circle that is owned by no one: its meanings can be imputed or inferred or interpreted but never controlled. And since stories and poems are much like Rorschach tests, they allow us to say important things about ourselves without really talking about ourselves, to speak indirectly about things that are hard to speak of directly. The shy soul is always grateful for opportunities to follow Emily Dickinson's advice: "Tell the truth, but tell it slant."

Take, for example, the first four lines of May Sarton's "Now I Become Myself," a poem we often use in the fall retreat to engage people with "the seed of true self":

> Now I become myself.
> It's taken time, many years and places.
> I have been dissolved and shaken,
> Worn other people's faces . . .

Even in those few lines, many people experience deep resonance with their own experience. The images draw us into a dialogue about how long it takes to become ourselves, how much turbulence we encounter along the way, and how often we mask ourselves in someone else's image, and yet they do so without demanding that we tell the difficult details of our journey.

Choosing good "third things" is an art. Good third things not only give shape to the dialogue but are worth being in dialogue about. Good third things are brief, accessible, and to the point, containing aspects of both the personal and the universal, allowing for exploration of the "little" stories of individuals while also encompassing larger archetypal themes. While we use some "tried and true" third things in our Courage to Teach retreats, formation is not curriculum-based, and facilitators are encouraged to discover and use poems and stories that have special meaning for them.

6. *Practicing the "clearness committee"*: The clearness committee is a method based on a centuries-old practice invented and used in the Quaker community to arrive at greater clarity or reach a place of discernment regarding a personal decision, issue, or dilemma. It is grounded in the dual beliefs that there are no external authorities on life's deepest issues but only the voice of truth that lies within each of us, and that we need community to help us avoid self-delusion as we listen for that voice.

In a clearness committee, a group of five or six people gather for the sole purpose of supporting the inner journey of a "focus person" who is struggling with an issue or dilemma. For two hours, committee members are prohibited from trying to advise, fix, save, or set this person straight. For two hours, they are allowed to speak to the focus person only by asking honest, open questions—questions that have no hidden agenda, questions that are not advice in disguise, questions that are not intended to lead in a certain direction—only questions that can help the focus person remove the blocks to inner truth and discover inner wisdom.

The benefits of this practice flow not only to the focus person; everyone who serves on a clearness committee learns much about deep listening—listening within themselves for the sources of good questions, listening for their own "fix-it" tendencies and attempting to hold them at bay, listening with respect to the unfolding of another human soul. Most people emerge from a clearness committee session having actually observed the inner teacher at work, often for the first time. This experience confirms that human beings have an inward source of authority that does not need to be supplied with imported "solutions" but needs only to be given a chance to speak and to be heard.

From Retreat to Schoolhouse to Educational Reform

What difference can a retreat program such as Courage to Teach make in the lives of K-12 educators, students, schools, and an entire system of public education that is in such deep difficulty?

In the course of offering this program, we have learned that the principles and practices of Courage to Teach are not limited to the hothouse atmosphere of the guarded and guided retreat. Teachers who participate in the program often take these principles and practices and adapt them for institutional use, frequently with promising results, as the following examples illustrate.

- A high school English teacher starts her departmental meetings by inviting a faculty member to open each meeting with a five-minute reflection on his or her passion for teaching English, or some current areas of "aliveness" in teaching. The result has been a much greater sense of connection and collegiality within the department, as they now have a space to share what brought them into the profession in the first place and what keeps them committed to it.

- An elementary teacher begins her fifth grade class each week with a "community circle," posing a reflective question to the group and creating a sense of safety for the children to speak about what is really on their minds and hearts so it can be heard by the other children.

- A middle school teacher actively introduces seasonal metaphors in her teaching, drawing on what is happening in the natural world and making connections to the human cycles of change that the seasons represent. By using stories of nature from different cultural traditions as well as poetry and art activities that highlight the deeper meanings of the seasons, she helps her students see their lives as part of a larger whole.

- A high school teacher introduces the concept of paradox to his class, explaining how two things that are seeming opposites can be understood as both/and rather than either/or. Students are encouraged to look at the many paradoxes in their own lives—such as dependent/independent, work/play, student/ teacher, thinking/feeling, active/passive—and then to consider the larger whole encompassed by these apparent polarities. In this way, the teacher introduces notions of complexity and wholeness and helps his or her students move beyond simplistic and dualistic thinking.

- A high school teacher works with students to help them identify their birthright gifts. Because it's often through the eyes of others that we recognize our own gifts, the students are asked to interview two of their friends, their parents and/or grandparents, or another trusted adult or teacher who knows them well. The interview questions are open-ended and evoke stories or anecdotes about the students' lives. Some questions relate to what the interviewees have noticed about the students—not just what they're good at but how they are in the world: what's important to them, how they interact with others, the kinds of roles they play with their family or friends. From these interviews and their own journaling, the students begin to construct their personal coat of arms, which includes a section on their birthright gifts.

- A group of teachers come together for collegial support not only to enhance good teaching but also to create a place for deeper dialogue about what it means to be a teacher. At each meeting one or two teachers are invited to present an issue or dilemma arising from their teaching, one that stands at the intersection of "soul" and "role." Using a modified clearness committee process, the other teachers respond by asking honest, open questions to help the individual uncover his or her own deeper understanding of this issue.

But the ultimate impact of the Courage to Teach program goes beyond committee and classroom into the complex arena of educational reform. Despite decades of reform initiatives, public schools remain "on the ropes" in too many communities around the country. Why do so many carefully planned efforts fail to achieve their well-intended outcomes? Why is it that many initially successful reforms have difficulty enduring, often losing ground as their champions become depleted by overwhelming demands? Why does public education struggle to find and keep good teachers in the increasingly complex and challenging public education environment?

Perhaps what is missing is what is most essential: sustained and heartfelt support for the people who are doing the work. For many, teaching is a calling, a vocation inspired by a passion to help others learn, by an ethic of service, and by a desire to make a positive difference. In teacher formation retreats, educators come together as colleagues, steadfastly reclaiming their identity and integrity as teachers. Enormous potential for positive change is rediscovered, and such change can result in greater depth and vitality in student-teacher relationships, renewed collegial practices in schools, and the revitalization of the teacher as leader in public education.

Two years after their Courage to Teach program had ended, we asked one group of participants how the experience had affected their personal and professional lives. To a person, what they told us reinforces our conviction that formation should be taken seriously as one avenue to educational reform:

> Courage is not a Band-Aid. It deals with the very core of the issue of education—the soul of the teacher. Without caring for the heartwood of a tree, the branches will fall off, the bark will peel and the roots will rot. Without caring for the soul, the teacher will become frustrated, ineffective and the students will fail. (Bonnie H., elementary school teacher, twelve years)

> How do you get people inspired and invested, willing and wanting to give their best, able to dig into their hearts and intellects for a cause? You value the teacher, in a way they trust and believe in. This is delicate territory. Courage to Teach explores and maps that territory. [CTT] has profoundly altered my comfort-discomfort continuum. I see my job as a treasure and an honor and am uncomfortable with less than my best. In short, I'm working harder and enjoying it more. What difference does this program make for students? In the beginning, my students are uncomfortable with the degree of earnest effort a class from me now requires. As time passe[s] they willingly, and with begrudging joy, "lean into" our tasks of learning. This program instigated a renaissance in my practice of teaching. I remembered my idealistic self. For a profession having difficulty retaining talented people, the importance is obvious. (John R., middle school teacher, twenty-five years)

> If public education is going to be a true road to a meaningful life and healthy community membership, we must nurture educators so they do not burn out and despair beneath overwhelming demands, but maintain an inner gyroscope and persevere. We all need to be more attentive to the needs of the soul—our own and that of children. Without this deeper perspective, all the well-meaning reforms will wither along with the teaching staff. We cannot do this work without replenishment. (Liz N., elementary school teacher, eighteen years)

If I don't know who I am or where I come from, I can't honor myself, be honored, or honor others. The honoring of teachers as individuals models the honoring [that] good teachers must demonstrate toward students in the classroom. Such respect and attention ultimately increases students' connection to school and learning. (Dana K., high school teacher, eight years)

Courage to Teach has enabled me to shift my lens from "what I need to do" to "what does this student need." It has reminded me that I teach human beings, not a subject matter. (David S., high school teacher, nine years)

A Partnership for Educational Reform

In 1993, when the staff of the Fetzer Institute, which supports Courage to Teach, began dreaming about a program that would affect teachers and schools in the ways described by the evaluations above, they knew from experience that there were some things they did not want to do. They did not want to confront school systems with a headlong run at reform. They did not want to develop and disseminate new teaching tools or techniques; teachers have methods aplenty to choose from and perhaps more consultants than they need. They did not want to produce written materials; such materials exist in abundance, but because of mandated curricula teachers have little time to use them. Instead, the Fetzer staff embraced the idea that teachers who cultivate their identity and integrity, their selfhood, will become both better teachers and more effective agents of institutional change.

Foundations often develop programs in an effort to change people's minds, hoping to cause a "great awakening" among those who slumber. But the instinct behind the Courage to Teach program is best expressed in the words of one of the Fetzer Institute's advisors: "Don't try to sell something to people who don't want it. Develop something of value that people already want, even if the people who want it are few in number."

This is the "remnant" or "leaven in the loaf" theory of change: there is power in working with felt needs, even if the qualities one is trying to encourage seem not to be shared by the masses, let alone by the elites. So the Fetzer staff launched the Courage to Teach program believing that it would not be for everyone. But they soon discovered that more professionals are ready for inner work than one might think.

In 1994, the Fetzer Institute sent a letter and two copies of a Courage to Teach brochure to a few dozen principals in Southwest Michigan, asking them to hand the materials to teachers who might be interested in a two-year pilot program. Many of the brochures were casually deposited in staff lounges, but teachers who were drawn to them made copies to pass on to their friends. In a very short time the institute received over eighty applications for twenty-five spaces, and it became clear that the problem would not be recruitment but selecting participants and expanding the program to accommodate even more. These "problems" have only compounded over the past six years with a program that has garnered enthusiasm, commitment, and funding from across the country.

The Fetzer Institute has not tried to market the Courage to Teach. Instead, program dissemination has followed a "movement" model of social change. Movements begin when a few individuals make the deeply inward decision to live "divided no more"—to live a life in which soul and role are joined, in which their external actions are congruent with their most cherished inner truths. As movements unfold, they develop communal structures to support those individuals in their common journey and to bring them into dialogue with others in the society who can help effect the needed change.

The Courage to Teach has been the Fetzer Institute's flagship program in applying the movement model by helping professionals do "soul work" in community. But the institute has experienced profound outcomes in every professional arena where this approach has informed our work, including medicine, science, law, diversity training, and the professional development of the institute's own staff.

From the outset of the program, the Fetzer staff has commissioned regular evaluations of the Courage to Teach program. These include two longitudinal studies of its effects on the lives of participants. Over a three- to five-year period, these studies have found the following:

- The Courage to Teach program rejuvenates teachers and renews their passion for teaching.
- Teachers believe that the experience improves their classroom practice in significant ways through the development of genuine connections with their students and a growing capacity to

"teach from the heart," and most feel that their students benefit tangibly from these changes.

- Most teachers feel that the program helps them develop more reflective habits in their teaching practice, and allows them to become more critical practitioners who can stop and reflect on their own teaching.

- Participants often find that their Courage to Teach experience leads them to initiate more collegial relationships when they return to their school site.

- Teachers who go through the program undertake new leadership roles in education, and often credit the program for their enhanced leadership skills, for their capacity to take new risks and confront new challenges.

- Most teachers feel that they live more mindful and balanced lives as a result of the Courage to Teach.

The coauthors of this chapter have collaborated with each other and many others around the country to create and sustain the Courage to Teach program. We take great joy in the work we are doing. But all of us involved in this program understand full well that we are not starting a movement but participating in one that has been gathering momentum for decades.

This movement—a movement to rejoin the powers of the human soul with the work we do in the world—is far more important than any one program. It is important because it promises to bring us greater fulfillment in the work we do. It is important because it promises to make us better colleagues. It is important because it promises to make us better teachers.

Above all else, this movement is important because it will help us serve the children well. Children need and deserve to be taught by adults who are in full possession of their own souls, so that they can help the young launch and live their lives from the center of healing and empowerment that exists within every human being.

ANGELES ARRIEN

The Way of the Teacher:
Principles of Deep Engagement

I have always been intrigued by the variety of ways that people of diverse cultures handle similar life experiences. It was my insatiable curiosity coupled with my desire to find a bridge between diversity and commonality that eventually led me into the field of cultural anthropology. This interdisciplinary arm of anthropology allowed me to study the history, art, philosophy, music, psychology, and religions of the peoples of the world. It is from this integrative approach that I have continued to look at the areas that every culture addresses in its own way: education, health care, family systems, governance, economics, communication, artistic expression, religion, and beliefs about the supernatural.

As we move into the twenty-first century, it is the work of all human beings to attend to the health of both our "inner" and "outer" houses: the inner house of our selves, the limitless world within; and the outer house of the world in which we live our daily lives. Many people in contemporary society feel little or no connection between these two worlds, a state that the indigenous, land-based peoples of the earth, whose cultures reach back thousands of years, would find not only sad but incomprehensible. I am grateful to my ancestors and family for providing me with a rich heritage. Through their history and pioneering Basque spirit, they have inspired me to stay connected with nature and to seek bridges between ancient origins and contemporary times.

To survive in the twenty-first century, we must become more adept at handling the waves of change that sweep our world faster than ever before. Essentially, the challenge for each individual is to become a master of change itself. The teacher today needs to be a good mentor and coach, and to help students develop the skills they will need to be the "change masters" of the future.

Individuals deal with change and support states of health through dreams, images, play, relationships, and acts of creative work. Cultures support change and states of health through these mythic structures and through the institutionalization of art, science, music, ritual, and drama. In cultures that are alienated from their mythological roots, renewal requires a return to the basic source from which all personal and cultural myths are ultimately forged—the human psyche.

In my research I have noted that many Native cultures draw on the power of four archetypes in order to live in harmony and balance with the environment and with our own inner nature: the Warrior/Leader, the Healer, the Visionary, and the Teacher. Because these archetypes spring from the deepest mythic roots of humanity, we too can tap into their wisdom. When we learn to live these archetypes within ourselves, we can begin to heal ourselves and our fragmented world.

The following four principles, each based on an archetype, embody what I call the Four-Fold Way, which can be used as a guideline for leading a life of quality and integrity. These principles form the core of deep engagement.

1. *Show up (or choose to be present)*. When we choose to be present, to become "visible," we are able, through example and intention, to empower and inspire others by what we model. We extend honor and respect, set limits and boundaries, and align words with actions. When challenges present themselves, we embrace them with full-bodied presence rather than pull away or constrict with fear. This Warrior/Leader principle guides us to be both firm and yielding, honoring our own individual limits and boundaries as well as the limits and boundaries of others.

Universally there are three kinds of power. In traditional societies people believe that if a person has all three powers, he or she embodies "big medicine."

- *The power of presence.* To some degree, every human being carries the quality of presence, which means that we are able to bring all four intelligences forward: mental, emotional, spiritual, and physical. Some individuals carry such presence that we identify them as charismatic or magnetic personalities. We are drawn to them, and they captivate our interest.
- *The power of communication.* Effective communication is accomplished through an alignment of content, right timing, and right placement. Communication that empowers and inspires us is communication that is delivered at the appropriate time and in the right place to be heard and received.
- *The power of position.* The leader demonstrates a willingness to take a stand. This power involves the capacity to let others know where one stands, what one stands for, and how one stands up for oneself.

2. *Pay attention (to heart and meaning).* It is the Healer's way to pay attention to what has heart and meaning, to open oneself to the possibility of removing the blocks and obstacles to receiving love and giving love. This principle guides individuals to observe where in their experience they are half-hearted rather than open-hearted, when they carry a doubting heart rather than a clear heart, and when they are experiencing weak-heartedness rather than strong-heartedness.

Cross-culturally, there are four universal healing salves: singing, dancing, storytelling, and silence. Important questions that enable individuals to assess the condition of their own states of health or well-being are: Where in my life did I stop singing? Where in my life did I stop dancing? Where in my life did I stop being enchanted by stories? and, Where in my life did I stop being comfortable with the sweet territory of silence? Attending to our own life stories allows us to experience the human resource of love, the most powerful healing force on Mother Earth.

3. Tell the truth (without blame or judgment). Many Native American cultures hold a belief that each individual is "original medicine" nowhere else duplicated on the planet, and therefore it is important to bring out each person's creative spirit and life dream or purpose on earth. Since we are "original medicine," there is no need for comparison and competition. The task is to come forward fully with our gifts, talents, and resources and to powerfully meet the tests and challenges of life.

The visionary is one who brings his or her voice into the world and refuses to edit, rehearse, perform, or hide. It is the visionary who knows that the power of creativity is aligned with authenticity. The field of creativity that exists within each individual is freed by moving out of ideas of wrong-doing or right-doing. If we can answer yes to the question, Is my self-worth as strong as my self-critic? then we are ready to engage in creative expression.

4. Be open to outcome (not attached to outcome). The process of learning and teaching is universal. Traditional societies believe that wisdom is flexible and fluid, never positional, that the human resource of wisdom is accessed by learning how to trust and how to be comfortable with states of not knowing. This principle is known as the Way of the Teacher.

Trust, Wisdom, and Detachment

The Way of the Teacher accesses the human resource of wisdom, and every culture has both traditional and nontraditional means of education. Whether they occur in an established school system or an apprenticeship, the processes of learning and teaching are universal. The Teacher has *wisdom*, teaches *trust*, and understands the need for *detachment*.

Mother Teresa recognized that it is the teacher's way to use trust as an instrument: "I feel like a pencil in God's hands. . . . God writes through us, and however imperfect instruments we may be, he writes beautifully. . . . He deigns to work through us. Is that not marvelous?"

It is the principle of the Teacher archetype that will help bring spirit into the schools. The principle that guides the Teacher is an openness to possibilities rather than an attachment to a particular outcome. The way of the Teacher is a practice in trust, which is the container out of which the qualities of wisdom grow: clarity, objectivity, discernment, and detachment. Wisdom is at work when we are open to all options.

Among indigenous peoples, it is considered foolish to take action during times of not knowing, and an act of wisdom to wait and trust. This kind of trust, however, can be a difficult skill to learn. The trickster archetype found in many of these traditional cultures functions as a teacher who shocks people into seeing their attachments and habitual patterns. Tricksters typically present surprises as a way of waking people up and forcing them out of their routines.

The opposite of trusting is trying to control the uncontrollable. An individual who has difficulty with surprises or the unexpected has attachments, fixed perspectives, and a strong need for control. Attachments are specific, immovable expectations, desires that are projected onto people, places, and situations. When we are "attached" in this sense of the word, we became controlling and rigid. The trickster reminds us to become more resilient and objective.

Most Westerners equate the word "detachment" with not caring, but the word is often defined in other cultures as "the capacity to care deeply from an objective place." When using the term here, we are speaking of what you might think of as nonattachment, letting go, maintaining our sense of humor. If we observe what causes us to lose our sense of humor, we can identify our point of attachment. When we don't get pulled in (or emotional), and when we maintain our sense of humor, we demonstrate our own capacity to care deeply from an objective place.

In the book *Leadership Is,* Harrison Owen writes of what he calls the immutable laws of the spirit: "Whoever is present are the right people to be there; whenever we start, it's always the right time; what happens is the only thing that could have happened; when it's over, it's over." Acceptance, rather than resignation, is the gift of detachment.

Ancestors

Across many cultures, people honor their ancestors as important teachers of detachment because they have faced the process of letting go and of experiencing the ultimate unknown, death. Indigenous people believe that the spirits of our ancestors literally stand behind us to support us in our life dream and purpose. Native people believe that what we do in this generation will affect seven generations to come. Anytime we don't act, the effect is the same.

It is important to consider in what ways we can bring forward the "good, true, and beautiful" that is in our heritage, and to know that the quality of our lives contributes to the opportunities and challenges for future generations to come. Many traditional societies classify "spiritual creatures" or ancestor spirits into three categories: ancestors who are our biological family; extended family and friends who are not related by blood, and figures in history who are sources of inspiration. These societies consider the spirits of "blood family" ancestors to be the most powerful for helping us to break harmful family patterns so that we can retain the good, true, and beautiful.

Empowerment Tools of the Teacher

The empowerment tools of the Teacher archetype include observing silence, calling the ancestor spirits for guidance, sitting meditation, and connecting with nature.

SILENCE

We can open to the Teacher archetype and the ancestor spirits through the healing salve of silence. In order to tap the human resource of wisdom, it is necessary to practice the art of listening. As Mark Twain put it, "A better idea than my own is to listen." Periods of silence and solitude allow us to obtain more clarity, objectivity, and discernment, the qualities inherent in wisdom.

CALLING THE ANCESTORS

Some traditions believe that calling the names of the ancestors will bring their help forward. The clicking of sticks or bones is another way to ask for ancestral help; each clicking sound represents our commitment to break harmful family patterns or harmful cultural patterns. For example, if alcoholism has been a harmful family pattern we have the opportunity to learn from the mistakes of our ancestors and to honor them by choosing not to extend the pattern forward ourselves.

SITTING MEDITATION

Sitting meditation teaches people how to wait, listen, and observe what is revealed. Sitting meditation teaches about the art of observation, where ideas and images are released as quickly as they are revealed. Other practices of detachment might include wilderness rope courses, river-rafting trips, rock climbing, high diving, and fishing—even bungy jumping.

CONNECTING TO NATURE

The principle teacher of detachment in nature is often Grandmother Ocean, who embodies flexibility and resilience. The West is the home of Grandmother Ocean and all the water creatures. It is from the West that Native peoples call forward the powers of silence, wisdom, and ancestral guidance. West is also associated with the season of fall, the time of harvesting or bringing in as well as letting go. The water creatures and Grandmother Ocean reveal our capacities for abundant harvest and unlimited fluidity, and indigenous cultures often hold water as sacred for its capacities to cleanse, nurture, heal, and purify. This reminds us that wisdom, like Grandmother Ocean, is always flexible and seldom rigid.

The Shadow Aspects of the Teacher

We experience the shadow side of the Teacher archetype when we find ourselves in states of righteous positionality, judgment, and control. The Teacher embraces these states, but does not indulge in them. The opposite of positionality is flexibility; the other side of judgment is objectivity and discernment; the opposite of control is trust. Patterns of positionality, judgment, and control are generally fear-based and always reveal a lack of trust. Universally, there are two sources of harm: fear and ignorance. Fear's major function is to alert us to something that may harm us so that we can heed the warning. Unfortunately, most of us feel fearful in a variety of situations that don't call for such protective measures. We do harm when we consciously ignore a person or a situation. We can also do unintentional harm in a state of "blissful ignorance."

CONFUSION

When we experience confusion, we should wait rather than act. If circumstances make it impossible not to act, we should seek pockets of clarity and act only in those areas.

ATTACHMENTS

The Teacher archetype requires us to balance our capacities so that we are as detached as we are attached. When we find ourselves overly attached to a particular outcome, our tendency is to control rather than to trust. When we are too attached to something, we often lose our objectivity about it, and thus our ability to do right by it. Wisdom is always flexible and seldom rigid. As we increase our capacities for flexibility, we increase our ability to express our wisdom and to let go of our attachments. By being open we may be able to find more creative solutions to life's dilemmas.

Following the Way of the Teacher

These exercises and questions will help you access the wisdom of the Way of the Teacher.

- Spend a portion of each day in solitude for the purpose of listening to your own knowing or wisdom. Set aside one full day a month to spend totally in silence.
- Spend some time honoring the richness of your roots and heritage. Collect pictures of important ancestors. Use these as visual reminders of the "good, true, and beautiful" aspects of your heritage.
- Ask yourself, Who have been the significant teachers in my life? Of these teachers, who were sources of inspiration and who were sources of challenge? What are the consistent qualities that I have been drawn to in these people? What does this reveal about my "inner teacher"? Who have I been a teacher for, and who do I currently hold as a mentor?
- Ask, Who are the trickster figures in my life who have taught me about flexibility and have revealed my patterns of position-

ality, judgment, and control? What "wake-up" calls have I experienced? How did I become aware of or "awaken to" limiting patterns that I have?

- Ask, What attachments do I find in my personal life? In my professional life? In my spiritual life?
- Ask, What life-negating family patterns am I consciously willing to break and no longer carry forward?
- Consciously make each day a focus for practicing wisdom. Ask yourself, How objective can I remain? Am I able to wait instead of act in times of confusion? Can I use discernment rather than judgment? Will I make decisions where I have clarity?
- On your birth date each month do something that you have never done before. Incorporating this monthly practice into your life increases your capacity to consciously approach the unknown and unfamiliar at least twelve times during the year.

In the context of a rapidly changing world, our society needs teachers who can empower children to become strong leaders, visionaries, and healers—teachers who can address basic questions about the well-being of the human spirit. Most traditional societies prepare their children through rites of passage, exposure and connection to nature, and time in silence, to promote character and integrity and enable young people to seek their dreams and bring their gifts and talents into the world in collaborative ways. Perhaps walking the Four-Fold Way means opening to the universal archetypes of the Warrior/Leader, the Healer, the Visionary, and the Teacher, which lie within us, waiting to express their wisdom in all of our actions and choices in the world.

Most traditional societies believe that the Warrior's Way is to know the right use of power, the Healer's Way is to extend love, the Visionary's Way is to express creativity and vision, and the Teacher's Way is to model wisdom. Through the resource of power we are able to show up. Through the resource of love we are able to pay attention to what has heart and meaning. Through the resource of vision we are able to give voice to what we see. And through the resource of wisdom we are able to be open to all possibilities.

Perhaps it is not a coincidence that the visionary poet William Blake wrote, "I in a fourfold vision see / And a fourfold vision is given me / Fourfold is my supreme delight . . ." When we open to being powerful, loving, creative, and wise, we experience the world and ourselves as the many splendid things that we are. This is the opportunity available to every teacher and student relationship, which can restore and sustain Spirit in our schools.

GEOFFREY CANADA

From *Fist Stick Knife Gun*

I returned to New York in 1983 armed with the experience of years of working with some of the toughest adolescents in Boston, my degrees from Bowdoin and Harvard, and my recently earned black belt in tae kwon do. I felt that because of my professional development in New England, and because of how I grew up, I was ready to come back to "prime time"—New York City—and make a difference.

I was hired by the Rheedlen Centers for Children and Families that summer. Rheedlen was then headed by Richard L. Murphy, who had founded the organization in 1970 as a truancy prevention program for children between the ages of five and twelve. Over the years Rheedlen's mission expanded with the expanding needs of poor children and their families, first to working with families, then to include an entire neighborhood. Richard Murphy, who would go on to be commissioner of the New York City Department of Youth Services under Mayor David N. Dinkins, had dedicated his life to saving poor children in Harlem and in other pockets of poverty on the west side of Manhattan. I recognized the same passion and commitment to poor children in him that I felt myself, and I was ready to go to work.

* * *

I remember feeling, when I first talked about coming to Rheedlen, that the job seemed perfect for me. But I raised one concern to Richard Murphy during the interview. I had to run a martial arts school. I explained that I had experimented with teaching inner-city kids martial arts in Boston as part of a violence reduction strategy, and that I was convinced that the discipline and values taught in martial arts could help young boys and girls resist the constant peer pressure to fight and act violently. I knew it seemed counter-intuitive that teaching young people how to punch, kick, and defend themselves would *reduce* violence, but I had seen firsthand the peace that many young people had experienced, some for the first time in their lives, after some time spent learning martial arts.

I thought that my insistence on teaching martial arts might prove to be a stumbling block to my taking the job at Rheedlen. But I was dedicated to reaching as many young people as I could, and I knew there was a certain segment of the population that I could only reach in this way. I remember how serious and solemn I was when I told Murphy all this. I mistook his smile for an indication that he thought it was a minor matter. He was smiling, in fact, because Rheedlen ran an afterschool program at a junior high school right down the block from our main offices and he thought it would be great to open a martial arts school right there, for the young people who lived in the neighborhood.

The director of the afterschool program was Joseph Stewart, a young man who had dedicated his life to serving the troubled youth in a very poor census tract of Manhattan known as Manhattan Valley. The junior high school where he ran his program was smack in the middle of Manhattan Valley and was named Booker T. Washington Junior High School 54. We all called it by its number, J. H. S. 54. Joe embraced my desire to offer a martial arts class there, and in September of 1983 I opened up the Chang Moo Kwan Tae Kwon Do Club in the school's basement.

My tae kwon do school is still at the junior high school, the classes have always been free, and I worry and fuss over my students like a mother hen. My fears for these boys and girls are grounded in a sad reality, one that sank in when I returned to New York and saw how drastically things were changing for the worse. After a very short time I realized that death circles over the ghettos of this country like a huge eagle, seemingly coming from nowhere, plucking our children from our midst suddenly and without notice.

When I look back on my first years at Rheedlen, I realize how clearly I saw the signs of what was coming. I began to try to get others interested in what I knew was an impending explosion of violence. But the violence hadn't yet crept out of our poor communities and into the more affluent neighborhoods around the country, and there seemed to be little outside interest in what those of us located in these communities began to dread—the end results of handguns in the hands of teenagers.

It's a Wednesday night in October and I can't believe I've gotten away from Rheedlen in time to be early for my martial arts class. In October and February I let new students into my classes and this class is full of them. I walk into the brightly lit gym and all eyes turn toward me. I'm walking with purpose, quickly and silently. A little boy begins to run over to me and an older student grabs his arm. I see him whispering in the younger boy's ear. I'm sure he's telling him, "You can't talk to him before class." And he's right. I talk to no one when I first come in to teach. One boy runs over and bows quickly and runs away. I nod my head in acknowledgment and continue my march to the tiny office that serves as my dressing room. I know that by now the word is out to all of the students that I'm teaching the class tonight.

In the quiet of my dressing room I begin to change into my uniform and I try to quiet my mind. It's harder than usual. The city is cutting youth services again. Rheedlen will be affected. This very night center will be closed unless I can raise the money privately to keep it open. That means more running around, more late nights, more lost weekends. That doesn't bother me, but it causes me to miss my classes. For eleven years I have taught martial arts in this school. For ten of those years I hardly ever missed a class. Now I'm lucky if I can make it one night a week. My three black belt students are good teachers, but they're young and still need my guidance.

I dress, leave the room, and go back into the gym. If you saw me now you might think I'm stern, even mean. No smile is on my face. I scan the room looking for any sign that my students are fooling around and not warming up the way they are supposed to. As my gaze travels around the room students stop playing tag and laughing and joking, and pretend that they're stretching or practicing their kicks. They hope I haven't seen them playing around, that they have fooled me. I pretend they have. I turn my back on them and silently go through my own drills, letting the tension and drama build. And suddenly I clap my hands two times and fifty children are dashing every which way trying to get in line. The older students have been waiting for this moment and know where to go, the younger students dart around trying to find an empty place in line. For a few moments it looks like everyone is playing a game of musical chairs.

I stand in front of them, looking unhappy and displeased. Everyone wonders who is out of place or not standing up straight. This is part of my act. Finally I begin the class and then I'm lost in the teaching. I'm trying to bring magic into the lives of these kids. To bring a sense of wonder and amazement. I can feel the students losing themselves and focusing on me. They are finally mine. I have them all to myself. I have crowded all the bad things out of their minds. The test they failed, the father who won't come by to see them, the dinner that won't be on the stove when they get home. I've pushed it all away by force of will and magic.

This is my time and I know all the tricks. I yell, I scream, I fly through the air with the greatest of ease. I take my black belt students and I slam them on the floor and they pop up like those weighted weeble dolls that can't stay down. I throw them through the air as if they were feathers, and they land and roll and are back up unhurt and unafraid. The new students can't believe their eyes. And they begin to believe in magic again.

And by the time the class is ending their eyes are wide with amazement and respect, and they look at me differently. And I line them up and I talk to them. I talk to them about values, about violence, about hope. I try to build within each one a reservoir of strength that they can draw from as they face the countless tribulations small and large that poor children face every day. And I try to convince each one that I know their true value, their worth as human beings, their special gift that God gave to them. And I hope they will make it to the next class with something left in that reservoir for me to add to week by week. It is from that reservoir that they will draw the strength to resist the drugs, the guns, the violence.

When class ends I dress, and now things are different. I speak to everyone. Students come up to shake hands and we bow in greeting. I am back to being Geoff to them, their friend. As a group of us walk up 108th Street together I scan the street for signs of danger. This, after all, is a neighborhood where more than ten adolescents have been killed by guns this year alone. I call one of the youngest students over to me. He is only five and comes to class with his older brother. I see that his jacket is open and I stoop down to zip it up.

The jacket is old and beat-up, probably belonged to his brother last year. The zipper is broken. He believes I can fix it. Why not? After watching me in class he believes that I can do anything. His face is filled with anticipation. It's cold outside and the long blocks he has to walk in the cold will seem shorter if I fix his jacket. I try to fix the zipper. I can't. Instead, I show him how to use one hand to hold his jacket closed close around his neck. I readjust his hand several times so he understands that there is a certain way to do it that meets my approval. This is also part of the act—all of the attention to detail keeps him from feeling ashamed. I notice his nose is running and take out the package of tissues that I keep in my pocket for just this purpose and wipe his nose. He doesn't object like most five-year-olds. He loves the care and concern. As I watch him cross the street with his brothers and friends, holding his jacket closed with his hand, the spell is broken for me. No more magic. Just little five-year-olds in raggedy jackets that won't close, trying to stay warm on a cold night. I scribble a note to myself to remember to find a way to get some jackets. Winter is coming.

My two black belts usually walk with me after class and stay with me until I catch a cab. I tell them it's not necessary, but they are there to make sure I get home all right. What a world. So dangerous that children feel that a third-degree black belt needs an escort to get home safely. The sad thing is, with all the guns and drugs in this community, they know I'm no safer than anyone else.

This community, like many across this country, is not safe for children and they usually walk home at night filled with fear and apprehension. But when I walk with them after class they are carefree, like children ought to be. They have no fear. They believe that if anything happens they'll be safe because I'm there. I'll fly through the air and with my magic karate I'll dispatch whatever evil threatens them. When these children see me standing on the corner watching them walk into their buildings they believe what children used to believe, that there are adults who can protect them. And because of that belief they see me as larger than life, like Superman or Batman. And I let them believe this even if my older black belts and I know different. Because in a world that is so cold and so harsh, children need heroes. Heroes give hope, and if these children have no hope they will have no future. And so I play the role of hero for them even if I have to resort to cheap tricks and theatrics.

And if I could get the mayors, and the governors, and the president to look into the eyes of the five-year-olds of this nation, dressed in old raggedy clothes, whose zippers are broken but whose dreams are still alive, they would know what I know—that children need people to fight for them. To stand with them on the most dangerous streets, in the dirtiest hallways, in their darkest hours. We as a country have been too willing to take from our weakest when times get hard. People who allow this to happen must be educated, must be challenged, must be turned around.

If we are to save our children then we must become people they will look up to. Children need heroes now more than ever because the poor children of this nation live with monsters every day. Monsters deprive them of heat in the winter, they don't fix their sinks and toilets, they let garbage pile up in their hallways, they kick them out of their homes, they beat them, shoot them, stab them—sometimes to death—they rape their bodies and their minds. Sometimes they lurk under the stairs. They scuttle around in the dark; you hear them in the walls gnawing, squeaking, occasionally biting a little finger.

We have failed our children. They live in a world where danger lurks all around them and their playgrounds are filled with broken glass, crack vials, and sudden death. And the stuff of our nightmares when we were children is the common reality for children today. Monsters are out there and claiming children in record numbers. And so we must stand up and be visible heroes, fighting for our children. I want people to understand the crisis that our children face and I want people to act.

LINDA LANTIERI

Epilogue:
The Challenge of Creating Schools
That Are Divided No More

*H*ow successful will we be in welcoming spirit into our secular schools? It will depend on how honestly those of us who are struggling to live an integrated life are willing to talk about and share our struggle with our skeptical colleagues. It will depend on whether after reading this book you will be inspired to bring your own human spirit more consciously into your teaching, wherever your classroom may be. Some of us will feel the tug to help others who yearn for a similar change. If that's you, welcome to the transition team—to the first day of the rest of your new life as a teacher living divided no more. But we've got a few challenges ahead of us in terms of giving this movement some momentum. Here's what we face.

We first have to continue to redefine what it means to be an educated person. This is a worldwide challenge to widen the vision of education beyond mastering a body of knowledge as measured on standardized tests. Even teachers who use our well-established Resolving Conflict Creatively Program are telling us that they are hanging on by a thread to make room for teaching our curriculum. Did you hear about the group of sophomores at Cambridge Rindge and Latin High School in Massachusetts who in the fall of 2000, on the day of their statewide mandatory assessment test, decided to commit an act of civil disobedience by choosing, despite the consequences for themselves and their school, to refuse to take the test? It may take our inner life of spirit activating our outer life of action to meet the challenge of widening our vision of education in the face of the current push toward standardization.

It will also help us to meet the educational field where it is by acknowledging that academics are and always will be important. The new vision of "soulful" education that we are talking about has the potential of producing students who not only have clear direction and purpose in life but are also emotionally and socially skillful, and academically competent as well. It is *not* an either-or situation and we have to communicate that.

The second challenge is for adults to let young people teach us how to bring soul into education. J. Robert Oppenheimer, one of the pioneers of nuclear energy, once said, "There are children playing in the streets who could solve some of the top problems in physics because they have modes of sensory perception that I lost long ago."[1] Innovation and transformational learning often come more easily to children and young people. Since children are interested in life's most basic questions, we need to allow and evoke what is already present in them. Our task as teachers is to remember how integrated young children's spirituality is and to find ways to protect it from being trampled on.

Sadly, as children move through our schools, they often receive spoken and unspoken messages that extraordinary experiences related to their inner lives are not honored as part of their reality. The older they become, the more repressed, forgotten, and locked within themselves these awarenesses and experiences become. Adolescence offers an opportunity to reopen this line of inquiry, yet young people at this stage are usually met once again with the adult tendency to ignore or trivialize transcendental experiences. What complicates matters is that few of us have experienced as learners the kind of holistic education we want to put into practice as teachers. We therefore need to actively seek out learning experiences for ourselves that embody the kind of education this book is addressing. My experience over a three-year period of being in community at the Fetzer Institute's Senior

Scholar and Fellows Program has provided me with a wonderful example of learning with the heart and spirit as well as the mind. I also meditate and pray daily and try to include in my life regular moments of being with silence and nature. If we hope to be part of bringing this work into schools, we will each need to create our own learning quests to find positive models and experiences of how to teach the whole person.

The third challenge we face in welcoming children's inner lives into our public schools is developing a common lexicon for how we talk about these things. How can we create common ground, including a new vocabulary for discussing the ultimate questions of meaning and purpose? For some of us, various words that were used throughout this book may have been an obstacle. Perceptions of what terms like "sacred," "inner life," "spiritual" mean are different for different people. We haven't yet developed an inclusive enough vocabulary to describe this realm of experience. We also need to find practices and approaches in the classroom that celebrate and respect the diversity of our individual religious and spiritual beliefs. We need to find ways to talk about these concerns that are as palatable to an evangelical Christian as to someone whose inner life is not defined by a specific religion. It will be important for schools and school districts to find consensus through a democratic process in which decision making includes those affected by the decision. It is only through building trust and truly listening to one another that fair guidelines can be developed for discussing matters of belief and values.

The fourth challenge is to root this work in scientific research, as well as in sound pedagogy and child development theory. Most child development theory focuses on personality development and on the emotional and intellectual realm; only rarely does it consider the spiritual or intuitive dimensions. However, recently we are seeing more and more studies that point to the benefits of nurturing children's spiritual development. Exploring this in a research-based context will be important. Current research in social/emotional learning and positive youth development has already begun to make this connection.

The fifth challenge is how to go about integrating the inner lives of students into the curriculum of a school district. I believe that this calls for a process very different from what we see happening in the prevention field or the field of social and emotional learning. In these fields, we institutionalize innovation through implementing promising practices and research-based programs that exemplify social and emotional learning in action, and we evaluate our success by carefully monitoring lessons and teaching strategies to "maintain integrity." To nurture children's spiritual development in schools, I don't think we will need to implement programs or create teacher's guides with prescriptive directions. Instead, this movement will rely on people— teachers, parents, principals who are committed to the idea of reaching the whole child and to the sustainable systemic change needed. I hope we won't write scripts that tell us the right things to say or do to evoke spirit in education. We will have to improvise and evaluate our effectiveness by means other than test scores. Practitioners will have to be the "change masters" Angeles Arrien talks about, designing, developing, and sharing flexible approaches to this domain. There will be a variety and fluidity to what we create.

And finally, as many *Schools with Spirit* authors have noted, we can't think about doing this work in classrooms without supporting the adults in children's lives in the nurturing of their own inner lives. Many of us want to help young people find deeper purpose and meaning, but we can't give what we don't have.

In *The Courage to Teach,* Parker J. Palmer writes, "We teach who we are."

> Teaching, like any truly human activity, emerges from one's inwardness. . . . As I teach, I project the condition of my soul onto my students, my subject, and our way of being together. . . . Teaching holds a mirror to the soul. If I am willing to look in the mirror and not run from what I see, I have a chance to gain self-knowledge. Knowing myself is as crucial to good teaching as knowing my students and my subject. When I do not know myself, I cannot know who my students are. I will see them through a glass darkly, in the shadows of my unexamined life—and when I cannot see them clearly, I cannot teach them well. When I do not know myself, I cannot know my subject—not at the deepest levels of embodied personal meaning.[2]

Soul work isn't about giving teachers a road map. This teaching must flow from the quality of each teacher's own inner life.

As we sense the power of the spiritual dimension in our schools, we may need to begin assessing how we are progressing. I offer the following self-assessment tool for organizing our thoughts about this domain. In asking ourselves these questions, we may begin to shed some light on the areas we can improve upon in order to more intentionally create schools with spirit. These questions can also be answered from the perspective of thinking about our homes or communities.

A SELF-ASSESSMENT QUIZ

1. Are you as connected as you would like to be with each individual child in your class?
2. Do you make time throughout the day to "be" with your students rather than engage in a specific "doing" activity?
3. Do the children in your class feel they are treated fairly and with love and respect by you and the other students?
4. Do you feel a sense of a larger purpose in terms of the specific work you are engaged in?
5. Do you feel appreciated for who you are in your work environment?
6. Are there opportunities throughout the school day to enjoy and notice beauty in an art form that makes everyone feel better inside?
7. Do you and your students have ample opportunity through studying history or through storytelling to honor the power of the past and our ancestors?
8. Do you provide regular classroom activities to explore and spend time in nature?
9. Do you and your students have a feeling of belonging to each other in which you can all take pride?
10. Do you and your students feel comfortable sharing thoughts about the deeper questions of meaning and purpose without having to find answers to those questions?
11. Does your classroom welcome children's beliefs and life experiences as they relate to their faith traditions or spiritual expressions?
12. Are there opportunities throughout the school day that spark creativity?

13. Do all students feel that they can be their genuine selves in the classroom?

14. Do you have particular classroom rituals that have meaning for everyone?

15. Are there forms of nature present in your classroom—plants, stones, etc.?

16. Is there enough free time in the school day?

17. Is there reflective silent time in the school day?

18. Is your classroom a place where people can change?

19. Are students eager to get to know children they don't already know?

20. Are there regular opportunities for students to be involved in volunteering or working on a social action project?

21. Does the school day have moments of spontaneity in which intuition redirects a discussion or an activity?

22. Do you and your students feel that most of what is being taught and learned is meaningful and useful?

Nel Noddings, educator and author of *The Challenge to Care in Schools,* beautifully sums up the kind of education we are advocating:

> I have argued that education should be organized around themes of care rather than traditional disciplines. All students should emerge in a general education that guides them in caring for self, intimate others, global others, plants, animals, and the environment, the human-made world and ideas. Such an aim doesn't work against intellectual development or academic achievement. On the contrary, it supplies a firm foundation for both.[3]

A window of opportunity exists right now in the field of education for soul to enter. The advocates of character education have provided a framework that respects the constitutional separation of church and state. We must use this opening to broaden this work even further.

I'm reminded of those often recalled words from the 1989 movie *Field of Dreams:* "If you build it, they will come." My hope is that the contributors to *Schools with Spirit* have communicated why it is worth taking this risk and that there are many different ways for schools to play an important role in awakening students to the possibility of living more integrated lives. We need to support and engage each other in this unfolding process.

Our mission is to insist that we develop policies and approaches that enable all our children to have their human spirits uplifted and their inner lives nourished as a normal, natural part of their schooling. It will take enormous courage and energy to work across the existing boundaries. Far from being marginal or irrelevant, attention to our inner life of mind and spirit will help us achieve the equilibrium we need in this chaotic world; we must foster the compassion, insight, and commitment to community that will be necessary to tackle the deep emotional, social, political, and spiritual dilemmas of our time.

As I look at the huge problems our young people will inherit—racism, poverty, violence, the degradation of nature—I can't imagine how we will make it if we leave soul out. My hope is that each of us finds a way to act to make sure that no child's soul is left behind and that every aspect of the human spirit is welcomed in our homes, communities, and especially our schools.

Finally, I would like to offer this invocation for the children of the future, written by Angeles Arrien.

> May you be powerfully loving and lovingly powerful; may you always have love be your guide with family, friends, and colleagues. Remember to listen carefully to your own heart and to the hearts of others.
>
> May you have the courage to always follow your dreams. Take an action every day to support your life dream, your love of nature, and your integrity.
>
> May you have the strength to overcome fear and pride, and instead follow what has heart and meaning for you.
>
> May you be guardians of truth, beauty, creativity, and laughter.
>
> May you protect, preserve, and care for nature and the wilderness.
>
> May you show respect to people of all ages and races, and help all living things keep their dignity.
>
> May you help to make a better world for the poor, the sick, the elderly, and the young by being an active, committed, and positive force in your community.
>
> May you value and maintain your health and the health and well-being of others.

May you respect all the ways human beings access their
   spirituality.

May you help create a global community committed to peace and
   nonviolence.

May you keep learning; ask questions, explore, discover, and
   always maintain curiosity and hope.

May you honor and respect diversity and the beauty and magic
   that occurs when differences join to create something far
   greater than one can imagine.

May you bring your gifts and talents forward every day without
   hesitation or reservation.

May you honor your ancestors and all those who have gone
   before you, for they have paved the way for you to do what
   you are here to do.

With deep gratitude and respect for all that you will do to make the
earth a better place in which to live.

Notes

Linda Lantieri / A Vision of Schools with Spirit

1. The Institute of Noetic Sciences, program brochure (1998), Sausalito, Calif., p. 1.
2. Dr. J. L. Aber and J. L. Brown, National Center for Children in Poverty at Columbia University's Joseph L. Mailman School of Public Health, *The Evaluation of the Resolving Conflict Creatively Program: Teaching Conflict Resolution, An Effective School-Based Approach to Violence Prevention* (New York: Columbia University, 1999).
3. Archbishop Desmond Tutu, remarks during the Hague Appeal for Peace International Conference, The Hague, Netherlands, May 12, 1999.
4. Annie E. Casey Foundation, *Kids Count Databook: State Profiles of Well-Being 1999* (Baltimore: 2000).
5. D. Shafer et al., "The NIMH Diagnostic Interview Schedule for Children," *Journal of the American Academy of Child and Adolescent Psychiatry* 35:865–77.
6. W. E. Loges and R. M. Kidder, *Global Values, Moral Boundaries: A Pilot Survey* (Comden, Maine: The Institute for Global Ethics, 1997).
7. Donna Uchida with Marvin Cetron and Floretta McKenzie, *Preparing Students for the Twenty-first Century* (Arlington, Va.: American Association of School Administrators, 1996), v.
8. Reported in the *Utne Reader* Nov./Dec. 2000, p. 78.
9. *Noetic Science Review* 47 (1998): 22.

10. H. Hodgkinson, "Demographics of Diversity for the Twenty-first Century," *Principal* 78 (September 1998): 26–34.

11. See U.S. Department of Education, "Religious Expression in Public Schools: A Statement of Principles," June 1998.

12. Search Institute, "The Asset Approach: Giving Kids What They Need to Succeed" (1997), 1–4.

13. James Garbarino, *Lost Boys: Why Our Sons Turn Violent and How We Can Save Them* (New York: Free Press, 1999).

14. Daniel Goleman, *Emotional Intelligence* (New York: Bantam Books, 1995).

15. Howard Gardner, *Intelligence Reframed: Multiple Intelligences for the Twenty-first Century* (New York: Basic Books, 1999).

16. Goleman, *Emotional Intelligence.*

17. Danah Zohar and Ian Marshall, *Spiritual Intelligence: The Ultimate Intelligence* (London: Bloomsbury, 2000).

18. David Hay with Rebecca Nye, *The Spirit of the Child* (London: Harper Collins, 1998).

Nancy Carlsson-Paige / Nurturing Meaningful Connections with Young Children

1. I teach graduate students in the School of Education at Lesley University in Cambridge, Massachusetts. I wish to thank the many students who have shared examples from their teaching experience with me and with others.

2. Here the student is referring to the concept of number tasks developed by the Swiss psychologist Jean Piaget, whose research and theoretical work gave teachers a way to understand a child's progression in constructing his or her own understanding of the logic and constancy of numbers.

3. Howard Gardner, *Frames of Mind: The Theory of Multiple Intelligences,* 10th anniversary ed. (New York: Basic Books, 1993).

4. Robert Coles, *The Spiritual Life of Children* (Boston: Houghton Mifflin, 1990); Thomas Armstrong, *The Radiant Child* (Wheaton, Ill.: Theosophical Publishing House, 1985).

5. Thank you to Vivian Delila Carlo for sharing her stories of Celín with me.

6. Rachael Kessler, *The Soul of Education: Helping Students Find Connection, Compassion, and Character at School* (Alexandria, Va.: Association for Supervision and Curriculum Development, 2000).

7. James Garbarino, *Raising Children in a Socially Toxic Environment* (San Francisco: Jossey-Bass, 1995).

8. Jean Piaget, *To Understand Is to Invent: The Future of Education* (New York: Grossman, 1973).

9. Kaiser Family Foundation, *Kids and the Media at the New Millennium: A Comprehensive National Analysis of Children's Media Use,* 1999.
10. A. Diamant, "Special Report: Media Violence," *Parents Magazine* 69 (1994): 40–41, 45.
11. Donald E. Cook, M.D., president, American Academy of Pediatrics; Clarice M. C. Kestenbaum, president, American Academy of Child and Adolescent Psychiatry; Michael Honacker, Ph.D., deputy chief executive officer, American Psychological Association; E. Ratcliffe Anderson, Jr., American Medical Association, "Joint Statement on the Impact of Entertainment Violence on Children," 26 July 2000 (statement released at Congressional Public Health Summit).
12. I am grateful to the teachers, written about here, who have shared their experiences and insights with me: Kirsten Howard, Stuart Lui, and Alison Wilson. William Kreidler was working as a staff developer for the year that I observed him in several classrooms. I will be forever grateful to Bill for his generosity as my first mentor in the field of conflict resolution.
13. Piaget described these characteristics of young children's thinking, commonly found in the age group from two to seven years.

Laura Parker Roerden / Lessons of the Wild

1. See Glenda Hanna, "Wilderness-Related Environmental Outcomes of Adventure and Ecology Education Programming," *Journal of Environmental Education* 27 (1995): 21.
2. David Orr, *Ecological Literacy: Education and the Transition to a Postmodern World* (Albany: State University of New York Press, 1992).
3. Ibid.
4. Sheldon Berman, *Children's Social Consciousness and the Development of Social Responsibility* (Albany: State University of New York Press, 1997).
5. Paulo Freire, *The Pedagogy of the Oppressed* (New York: Continuum, 1990).
6. Richard Nelson, *The Island Within* (New York: Vintage Books, 1989).

Zephryn Conte / The Gift of the Arts

1. William Glasser, *Control Theory* (New York: Harper & Row, 1984).

Rachael Kessler / Soul of Students, Soul of Teachers

1. See Ira Progoff, *At a Journal Workshop: The Basic Text and Guide for Using the* Intensive Journal *Process* (New York: Dialogue House Library, 1975).
2. Michael Meade, *Men and the Water of Life: Initiation and the Tempering of Men* (San Francisco: Harper, 1993), 19.

3. See Jack Zimmerman and Virginia Coyle, *The Way of Council* (Las Vegas, Nev.: Bramble Books, 1996).

4. See Thich Nhat Hanh, *Being Peace* (Berkeley, Calif.: Parallax Press, 1987).

5. D. M. Dooling, "Focus," in *Parabola,* spring 1990.

6. Chogyam Trungpa, *Shambhala: The Sacred Path of the Warrior* (New York: Bantam Books, 1984), 71.

Epilogue

1. Quoted in Marshall McLuhan and Quentin Fiore, *The Medium Is the Message* (New York: Bantam, 1967), 93.

2. Parker J. Palmer, *The Courage to Teach* (San Francisco: Jossey-Bass, 1998).

3. Nel Noddings, *The Challenge to Care in Schools: An Alternative Approach to Education,* 3d ed. (New York, Teachers College Press, 1995), 679.

Contributors

ANGELES ARRIEN is an anthropologist, educator, and award-winning author. She is also a consultant and keynote presenter to organizations, corporations, and academic institutions such as the Fetzer Institute, the California Pacific Medical Center, the Kellogg Foundation, Hewlett-Packard Labs, Wharton Business School, the University of California system, and the California Institute of Integral Studies. She is president of the Foundation for Cross-Cultural Education and Research, and a fellow of the Institute of Noetic Sciences. She lives in the San Francisco Bay area. For further information on products and programs visit www.angelesarrien.com or write to Angeles Arrien, P.O. Box 2077, Sausalito, CA 94966.

LARRY BRENDTRO is president of Reclaiming Youth International, a nonprofit organization providing training and research on challenging youth. He has been a teacher, principal, psychologist, and professor at the University of Illinois, Ohio State University, and Augustana College. He also directed Starr Commonwealth, which serves troubled youth in Michigan and Ohio. He currently coedits the journal *Reclaiming Children and Youth*. He was adopted into the Lakota Rosebud

(Sioux) tribe by the family of Noah and Anna Brokenleg. His ceremonial name is Mato Mani (Walking Bear).

MARTIN BROKENLEG is professor of Native American studies at Augustana College in Sioux Falls, South Dakota, and dean of the Black Hills Seminars on Reclaiming Youth. He is also a graduate of the Episcopal Divinity School of Cambridge, Massachusetts, and has been a substance abuse counselor, prison chaplain, and therapist for troubled youth. He has trained professionals worldwide, and his publications include *Reclaiming Youth at Risk,* coauthored with Larry Brendtro and Steve Van Bockern. For further information on the Circle of Courage or Reclaiming Youth International visit www.reclaiming. com or write to Circle of Courage, P.O. Box 57, Lennox, SD 57039.

GEOFFREY CANADA is president of the Rheedlen Centers for Children and Families (www.rheedlen.org) in New York City. He is the recipient of a Heinz Foundation Award and a *Parents Magazine* Award for his work in child advocacy, among many other honors. He is the author of *Fist Stick Knife Gun* and of *Reaching Up for Manhood: Transforming the Lives of Boys in America.*

NANCY CARLSSON-PAIGE is a professor at Lesley University, where she teaches courses in early childhood education and conflict resolution. For more than fifteen years, Nancy has been studying children's social development, the influence of media violence on children, and how children learn positive skills for getting along and resolving their conflicts. Nancy has coauthored four books and many articles on topics that relate to how children learn violent attitudes and behaviors, and about how they learn the skills of peacemaking and conflict resolution. She cofounded, along with Linda Lantieri, the master's degree program in Conflict Resolution and Peaceable Schools at Lesley University. For more information on the Center for Peaceable Schools go to www.lesley.edu.

ZEPHRYN CONTE is an artist, educator, and professional development specialist with Educators for Social Responsibility. She has taught children K-12 and trained adults for over twenty years. She has designed and implemented several programs in the arts and community building, the most recent a National Endowment for the Arts initiative, "The Art in Peacemaking." She has written arts curricula and facilitative leadership guides, including *The Road to City Center* and *ArtPeace;* is coauthor of *Cayenne,* a book of performance poetry; and has won special music awards from ASCAP (American Society of Composers, Authors and Publishers). She can be reached through Environarts, Inc., P.O. Box 2458, Tempe, AZ 85280 (www.environarts-inc.com); or at evirnarts@aol.com.

MARCY JACKSON codirects the national Center for Teacher Formation, leads Courage to Teach programs in Washington State, and facilitates formation retreats across the country. She has twenty years of experience as a child and family therapist, group facilitator, teacher, and retreat leader.

RICK JACKSON codirects the national Center for Teacher Formation, leads Courage to Teach programs in Washington State, and facilitates formation retreats across the country. Rick has been an executive with the YMCA for twenty-five years. He also consults to nonprofits and foundations on leadership, youth, and community formation.

RACHAEL KESSLER is director of the Institute for Social and Emotional Learning, which provides staff and curriculum development that infuse heart, spirit, and community throughout school life and learning. She is the author of *The Soul of Education: Helping Students Find Connection, Compassion, and Character at School* and coauthor of *Promoting Social and Emotional Learning: Guidelines for Educators.* She can be reached at selrachael@aol.com. For further information, visit www.mediatorsfoundation.org/isel or write 3833 North 57th Street, Boulder, CO 80301.

LINDA LANTIERI is a Fulbright scholar and internationally known keynote speaker with over thirty years of experience in education as an elementary school teacher, middle school administrator, and university professor. Currently she is the founding director of one of the country's largest research-based K-12 school programs in social and emotional learning, the Resolving Conflict Creatively Program, an effort of Educators for Social Responsibility. She also serves in a leadership capacity for the Collaborative to Advance Social and Emotional Learning and is the coauthor of *Waging Peace in Our Schools* (Beacon Press, 1996). She is the recipient of many awards and honors, including the Richard R. Green Distinguished Educator Award; she has been a senior scholar at the Fetzer Institute; and she was honored as an educational innovator by the National Education Association. For further information, contact the RCCP National Center at 40 Exchange Pl., Suite 1111, New York, New York 10005, or Llantieri @worldnet.att.net; or visit www.casel.org or www.esrnational.org.

JACOB NEEDLEMAN is a professor of philosophy at San Francisco State University and former director of the Center for the Study of New Religions at Graduate Theological Union. He was educated in philosophy at Harvard, Yale, and the University of Freiburg, Germany. He has also served as a research associate at the Rockefeller Institute for Medical Research and was a research fellow at Union Theological Seminary. He is the author of *A Little Book on Love, Money and the Meaning of Life, The New Religions, A Sense of the Cosmos, Lost Christianity, The Heart of Philosophy, The Way of the Physician,* and *Sorcerers* (a novel), and was general editor of the Penguin Metaphysical Library. In addition to teaching and writing, he serves as a consultant in the fields of psychology, education, medical ethics, philanthropy, and business, and is increasingly well known as an organizer and moderator of conferences in these fields. He has also been featured on Bill Moyers's acclaimed PBS series *A World of Ideas.* His most recent book is *Time and the Soul.* He can be contacted through the Department of Philosophy, San Francisco State University, San Francisco, CA 94132, or at Jneedle@sfsu.edu.

PARKER J. PALMER is a writer and traveling teacher who works on issues in education, community, spirituality, and social change. The Leadership Project named him as one of the thirty "most influential senior leaders" in higher education and one of the ten key "agenda-setters" of the past decade. His most recent book is *Let Your Life Speak: Listening for the Voice of Vocation.* For further information about Courage to Teach, visit www.teacherformation.org.

LAURA PARKER ROERDEN is a writer and environmental educator,

and the director of Ocean Matters (formerly the Northfield Mount
Hermon Summer Marine Biology Program). She has taught children
in grades four through twelve in settings as varied as traditional class-
rooms, the deck of a ship, and a hundred feet beneath the sea. She is
the author of several educational texts promoting children's social,
emotional, and ethical development, including *Don't Laugh at Me,
Net Lessons: Web-Based Projects for Your Classroom,* and *A Summer of
Service,* and is a contributing author, with William J. Kreidler, of *Early
Childhood Adventures in Peacemaking.* She lives and works in Boston.
She can be reached through Ocean Matters, 535 Albany Street, Boston,
MA 02118 (www.oceanmatters.org) or at lproerden@oceanmatters.
org.

DAVID SLUYTER is executive vice president and CEO of the Fetzer Institute, a foundation that investigates the implications of mind-body-
spirit unity. His work includes creating programs for teachers, health
professionals, and other public leaders. He received his doctorate
from Western Michigan University in counseling psychology and held
a number of leadership positions in mental health organizations before coming to the Fetzer Institute.

Acknowledgments

*W*hen I said yes to Beacon Press's generous offer to publish *Schools with Spirit*, I knew only that I was to be the instrument to help this book happen. It took a big leap of faith into the unknown. Luckily, when I landed I was met with an abundance of support and the resources to make all this possible. I would like to acknowledge the following loving spirits.

Thank you first and foremost to my friend and colleague Laura Parker Roerden, who discerned early on how deeply involved she needed to be to make this book happen. Without her ability to bring order and coordination to the project and turn my handwritten pages into polished manuscripts, I could not have completed this task. This brief mention of her name hardly does justice to the size of her contribution. And thank you, Joy Sumberg, for being Laura's support.

I also extend here my gratitude to all the authors who generously shared of themselves and their time to write chapters for this book and so to help bring forth a soulful vision of education.

I am thankful for the support of Elaine Seiler, Eileen Rockefeller Growald, and Ed Skloot and Robert Sherman of the Surdna Foundation, who believed I could tackle this topic in the first place and whose loving encouragement and financial support gave me the courage to try.

My gratitude also to the Marion Foundation, whose members and friends are dedicated to connecting people to one another in circles of interest and meaning. Thank you for supporting the next phase of getting this message out into the wider community.

My gratitude to all those at Beacon Press who made this book a reality, especially executive editor Deanne Urmy, whose unshakable support, integrity, and deep insight got me through another book. Thank you for always honoring my process.

Thanks also to all those with whom I have a spiritual kinship and are a part of my soul family, especially the 1998–2001 Fetzer Fellow and Senior Scholar community: "somebody prayed for us and had us on their minds." I am eternally grateful that we have found each other.

I also received help and support from my work colleagues, particularly the Resolving Conflict Creatively family, especially Nikki Ramsey and Catherine Rowe, the Collaborative to Advance Social and Emotional Learning, Reclaiming Youth International, Operation Respect, and Lucy Lopez-Roig and Associates. Thank you.

I am also grateful for the powerful team of family and friends too numerous to mention who are a constant source of spiritual strength and support, especially my soulfriend Carmella B'Hahn, who shares a mutual commitment to the growth of our sacred quest and spiritual development.

And finally, thank you, God. I know you haven't finished with me yet.